50 Ways to Paint a Wall

50 Ways to Paint a Wall

The Easy Step-by-Step Way to Decorator Looks

Gail E. McCauley

Creative Publishing international
Chanhassen, Minnesota

Copyright © 2005
Creative Publishing international
18705 Lake Drive East
Chanhassen, Minnesota 55317
1-800-328-3895
www.creativepub.com
All rights reserved

Creative Publishing
international

President/CEO: Ken Fund
Vice President/Publisher: Linda Ball
Vice President/Retail Sales: Kevin Haas

50 WAYS TO PAINT A WALL

Executive Editor: Alison Brown Cerier
Managing Editor: Yen Le
Senior Editor: Linda Neubauer
Stylist: Joanne Wawra
Photographer: Tate Carlson
Page Design: Brad Springer
Production Manager: Helga Thielen

Cover Design: Laura Shaw
Painter: Adele Satori

Contributors: Melanie Royals for information on dimensional
stenciling. Bestt Liebco (www.paintbrushes.com) for all the faux
finishing tools.

Library of Congress Cataloging-in-Publication Data
McCauley, Gail E.
  50 ways to paint a wall : the easy step-by-step way to decorator
looks/ Gail E. McCauley.
      p. cm.
  ISBN 1-58923-168-6 (soft cover)
  1. House painting. 2. Interior decoration. I. Title: Fifty ways to
paint a wall. II. Title.
  TT323.M38 2005
  747'.3--dc22

                              2004028208

Printed in China:
10 9 8 7 6 5 4 3 2 1

ABOUT THE AUTHOR

Gail E. McCauley is an expert on
trends in decorating with paint. She
has written for regional and nationally
syndicated shelter publications, as
well as paint organizations and web
sites that provide information to
consumers and the media. Gail lives
in Scottsdale, Arizona.

Contents

10   **Choosing One**

12   **Decorative Techniques**

44   **Geometric Designs**

64   **Faux Finishes**

100   **Wall Embellishments**

120   **Painting Basics**

       All About Paint   120

       The Right Tools   122

       Preparing the Surface   123

       How to Paint   127

50 Ways to Paint a Wall

Decorative
TECHNIQUES

1 Color Washing

2 Overlaying Color

3 Sponging

4 Ragging

5 Double Rolling

6 Dragging/Strié

7 Color Weaving

8 Combing

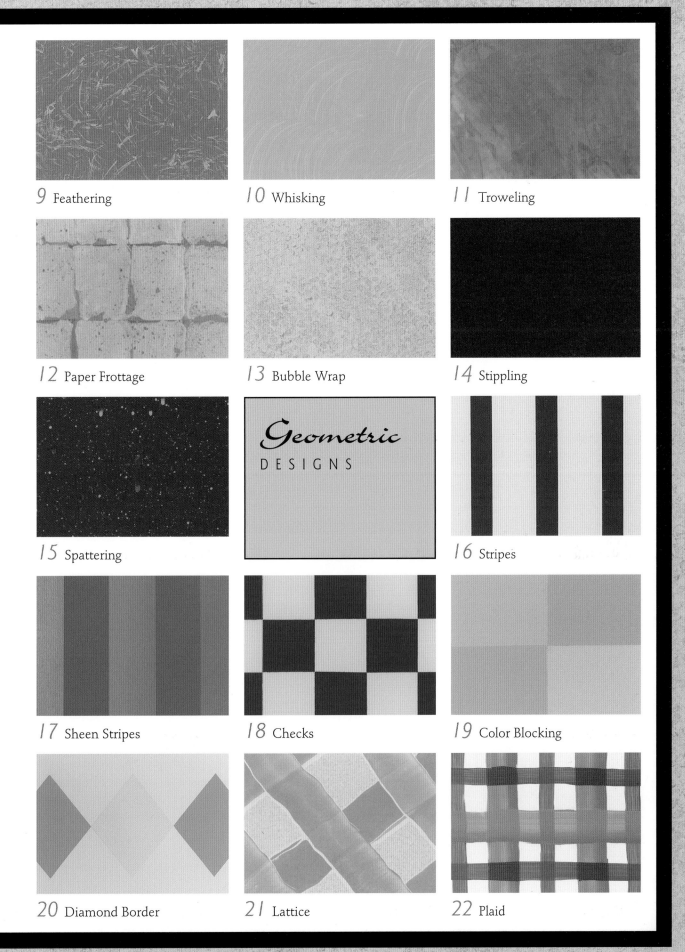

9 Feathering

10 Whisking

11 Troweling

12 Paper Frottage

13 Bubble Wrap

14 Stippling

15 Spattering

Geometric DESIGNS

16 Stripes

17 Sheen Stripes

18 Checks

19 Color Blocking

20 Diamond Border

21 Lattice

22 Plaid

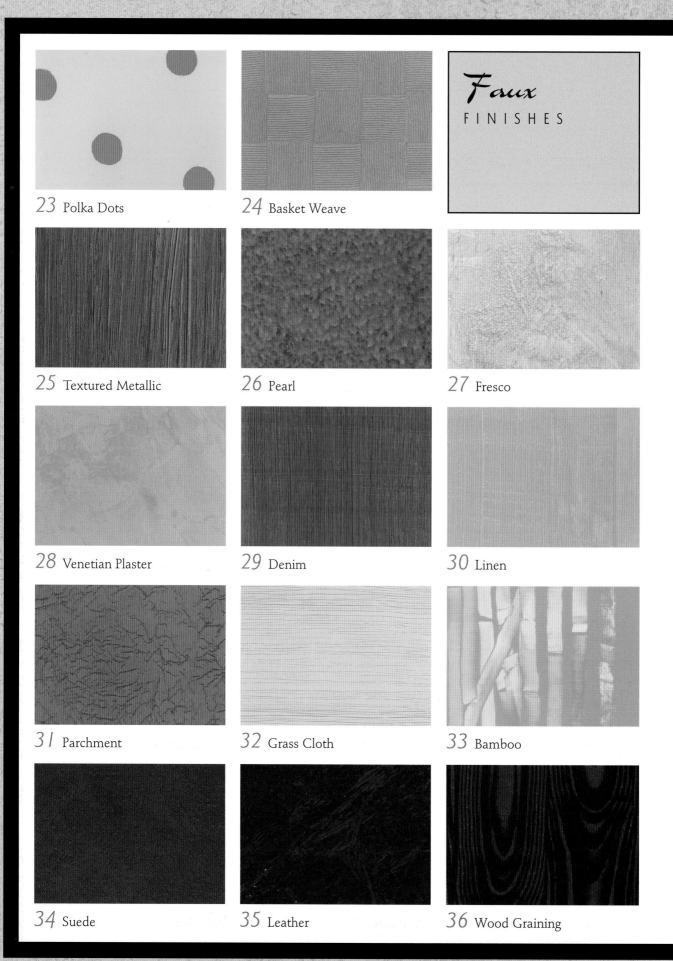

Faux
FINISHES

23 Polka Dots

24 Basket Weave

25 Textured Metallic

26 Pearl

27 Fresco

28 Venetian Plaster

29 Denim

30 Linen

31 Parchment

32 Grass Cloth

33 Bamboo

34 Suede

35 Leather

36 Wood Graining

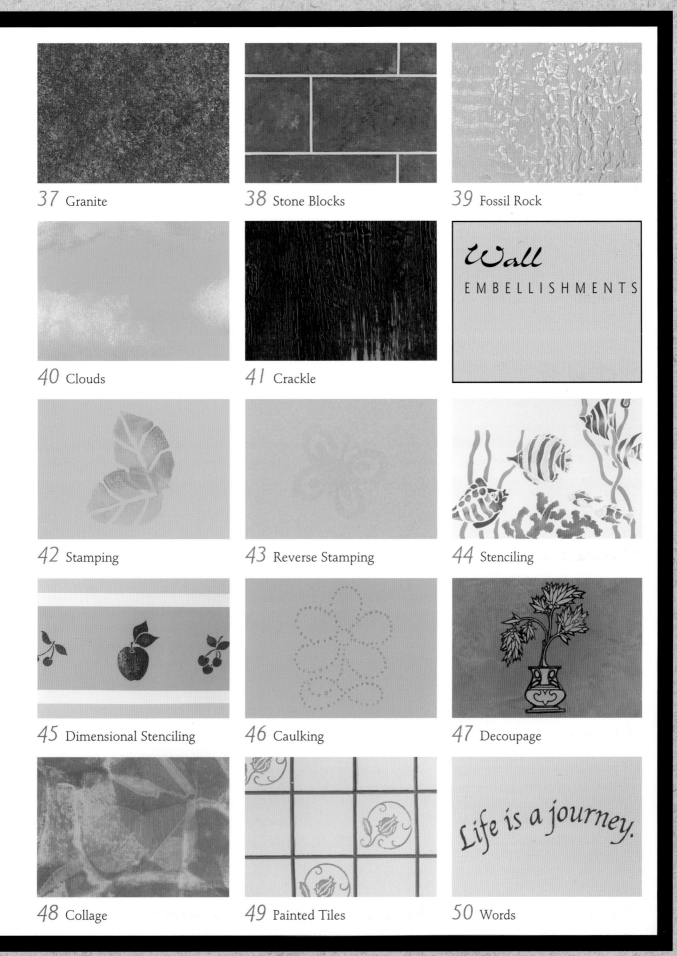

37 Granite

38 Stone Blocks

39 Fossil Rock

40 Clouds

41 Crackle

Wall EMBELLISHMENTS

42 Stamping

43 Reverse Stamping

44 Stenciling

45 Dimensional Stenciling

46 Caulking

47 Decoupage

48 Collage

49 Painted Tiles

50 Words

Life is a journey.

Choosing One

Today's decorative paint techniques will transform any room with their intriguing patterns, tantalizing colors, and rich textures. *50 Ways to Paint a Wall* shows how you can work this magic yourself. The fifty ways include techniques using special applicators, faux finishes that mimic everything from stone to cloth, bold geometric designs, and a variety of wall embellishments. You can achieve a range of looks with each method simply by varying the paint colors or applicators.

Although some techniques require special paint tools, many require only an ordinary paintbrush and roller or common items (for example, bubble wrap!). Follow the instructions and photos and you will be successful even if you have no experience with painting. At the back of the book is a basics section covering types of paint, wall preparation (which is important), and basic brushwork and rollering.

With fifty options, how will you choose the paint technique that is just right for your next decorating project? The introductions for each technique give decorating tips and practical information that will help you decide.

CONSIDER THE DÉCOR

There are elements that must be incorporated into your plan: the room's architectural features, the amount of natural light, floor covering and furnishings that will stay the same. Less tangible but equally important is the mood you want to create.

While the techniques will complement a variety of room décors, many seem particularly well suited to certain styles, and the introductions will tell you when that's so. For example, an iridescent finish, such as textured metallic or pearl, can be teamed with sleek furnishings for a sophisticated, contemporary look. Techniques that look like natural surfaces, such as stone blocks, granite, fossil rock, and bamboo, create an earthy ambience well suited to rustic country or Southwestern interiors. Faux finished walls that look like grass cloth, suede, leather, linen, or denim can work with a variety of décor styles, from retro to ultramodern. They are as

much at home among patriotic Americana as they are in ethnically inspired spaces. Classic paint techniques that emphasize patterns like diamonds and stripes are particularly at home with traditionally styled architecture and furnishings. Burgundy sheen stripes can lend grandeur to the walls of a formal dining room. Walls painted to look like rich leather bring classic sophistication to a home office or study.

The more subtle techniques produce a background for small spaces and for rooms where you want the walls to blend with existing décor. Geometric designs and wall embellishments produce obvious patterns more suitable for larger spaces where they complement (rather than overwhelm) the area; they are also perfect for small wall spaces and accent walls.

Paint techniques can draw attention to architectural elements, such as pillars, niches, alcoves, or built-in shelving, or create a focal point wall in an otherwise ordinary room. On the other hand, you can unify an open-concept living space with the same or coordinating paint treatments on the walls.

SELECT COLORS

Besides picking a technique, you have to pick the color. Colors are extremely powerful. They affect our emotions and energy levels and even influence our perceptions of space and temperature. Reds, yellows, and oranges are the warm colors. They are cheerful and uplifting; they energize and stimulate us. When painted with warm colors, walls seem to advance, making a large space cozier. Blues, greens, and violets are the cool colors. They are calming and relaxing, making them popular choices for bedrooms and bathrooms. The cool colors tend to recede visually, making a small area appear more spacious.

Pure, saturated colors are clear and bright and energize a room. Muted colors have a calming effect and impart an air of sophistication. These include neutrals, such as the grays, beiges, and tans.

The lightness or darkness of a color (its "value") makes a big difference, too.
• Light, or pastel, colors are soothing and gentle. Dark and bold colors are dramatic.

- A mixture of light, medium, and dark values in a room creates interest by keeping the eye moving from one area to another.
- Combining light and dark colors intensifies the effect of both colors and creates drama. Painting the short end walls of a long, narrow room darker than the long side walls creates the illusion that the room is more square.
- Any color appears more intense next to white. If you want to boost a soft pastel pink in a girl's bedroom, for example, paint the woodwork white.

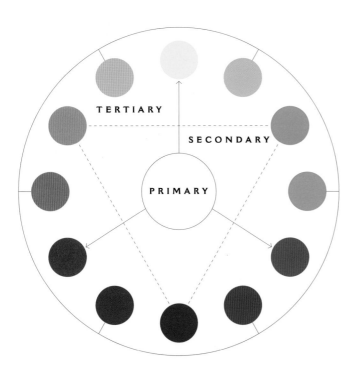

A color wheel is a great tool for developing color combinations. Here are some of the basic color schemes you can use in your home:
- Monochromatic schemes include various values of the same color. These combinations are subtle, sophisticated, and calming.
- Complementary colors (those that are opposite each other on the color wheel) make each other appear more intense. For the best effect, use more of one color than the other, allowing one color to dominate and the other to accent the room.
- Analogous color combinations include hues that appear next to each other on the color wheel. They harmonize naturally.
- Triadic schemes include colors located equal distances apart, such as the three primary colors, red, blue, and yellow, or the three secondary colors, green, orange, and purple.

Always try color samples on the wall first, in both natural and artificial light. Rooms that receive indirect light, such as from a northern exposure, benefit from brighter, bolder colors. Direct sunlight that enters the room from the south can intensify colors and add a subtle yellow tone. Incandescent light brings out the warm colors in a room, and fluorescent lights emphasize cool colors.

Some techniques are usually created in particular colors, which the introductions will note. For example, both denim and the sky behind fluffy clouds are traditionally blue.

Above all, choose colors you enjoy. Rather than adopting a color scheme just because it's trendy, gravitate toward colors that have been your favorites for a long time. Don't be afraid to be bold with color. No more white walls!

PRACTICAL CONSIDERATIONS

How much time do you want to spend? Some paint techniques are quick to finish, while others have more steps, perhaps with drying time between each one. Also, a few decorative paint techniques, including fresco, Venetian plaster, collage, and fossil rock, result in raised surfaces that cannot be changed with a simple coat of paint. You will have to replace the plasterboard to successfully remove them. Think of them for small, isolated areas. Most techniques can easily be painted over, though, which is a reason to be bold and try something new.

HAVE FUN

If this is your first experience with decorative painting, it's fine to start small. Expand your paint horizons by introducing surprising color, design, or texture to one wall. If you are satisfied with the results, consider taking on a larger decorative paint project next. Why not add dimensional color and pattern to a narrow hallway, small front entry space, or dark kitchen? When you see the results, you'll be looking for more walls to paint. Experiment with paint and add your own touches. The possibilities are endless!

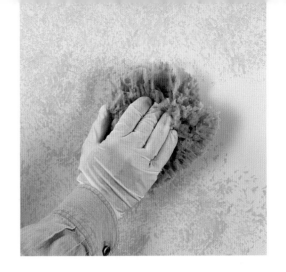

Decorative TECHNIQUES

The fifteen painting techniques in this section transform walls with interesting visual textures. Some involve the application of paint using unique methods or tools. For others, paint or glaze is manipulated on the wall to create distinctive patterns and decorative effects.

1 Color Washing

COLOR WASHING gives walls a subtle, watercolored appearance. Using a wide paintbrush, a translucent paint glaze is applied over a base coat in simple, crosshatch strokes, leaving a finish that has soft texture and color depth. Flat, smooth walls can be color washed to add visual dimension. The rough texture of a plaster or stucco wall is amplified by color washing.

This versatile finish is commonly used for rustic and country styled interiors and for casual spaces, such as family rooms, dens, and kitchens. Color washing provides a more interesting background for stenciled or stamped designs than a plain painted wall. It is also an effective way to "age" the walls of new homes or to mellow a painted wall that turned out brighter or bolder than expected.

The color-washing glaze can be either lighter or darker than the base coat color. The farther apart the base coat and glaze are in value, the more pronounced the effect. Often white or off-white is used for either the base coat or glaze. You can also use two tones or shades of the same color. Two different colors will blend together—yellow over blue will turn green. The glaze coat color will be the strongest.

MATERIALS AND TOOLS

- ❖ Painter's masking tape
- ❖ Drop cloths
- ❖ Paint roller and tray
- ❖ Satin or semigloss latex paint for base coat
- ❖ Rubber gloves
- ❖ Water-based glazing liquid
- ❖ Flat latex paint for top coat
- ❖ Paint bucket and mixing tool
- ❖ Paintbrush, 4" to 6" (10 to 15 cm) wide

1 Prepare the walls for painting (page 123). Protect the area around the walls with painter's masking tape and drop cloths (page 126). Apply the base coat and let it dry completely.

2 Put on rubber gloves. In the bucket, prepare the glaze, mixing four parts glazing liquid with one part top-coat paint. If you want a more translucent glaze, add some water.

3 Beginning in a top corner, brush the mixture over a 3-ft. (1 m) square section with a crosshatch or "X" motion. Go over the area several times, lightly blending the strokes. There will be light lines in the finish (they will be less visible if the wall is textured).

4 Immediately move to an adjacent section and repeat step 3. While the glaze from the previous section is still wet, blend the areas together. Work from corner to corner, moving down toward the floor in small sections until you have color-washed the entire wall. Allow the wall to dry completely.

5 If desired, repeat steps 2 to 4 with a lighter or darker shade of glaze to give the wall more depth.

2 Overlaying Color

THIS IS AN EASY technique for even the first-time decorative painter because it doesn't require skillful handling of a paintbrush or other tools. Paints are dabbed onto the wall with a wad of cotton knit fabric called "jersey." Every pounce of the cloth produces a soft, textured imprint. As more color layers are applied, the imprints blend together, building texture and depth. Because of its complex, dappled appearance, overlaying color disguises any surface flaws and an errant stroke can simply be dabbed over.

The size and "landscape" of the scrunched cotton jersey determine the finished look. Large, loosely scrunched pieces of fabric produce a coarsely textured appearance, suitable for bedrooms, family rooms, and casual areas of the home. Smaller, tightly wadded fabric produces a finer-grained, more controlled texture, appropriate for the dining room, living room, home library, and other formal living areas.

For best results, select a light, neutral hue for the base-coat color. Select the overlay colors to coordinate with the room furnishings. Choose a light and dark value of the same color or of colors that are close to each other on the color wheel.

MATERIALS AND TOOLS

- ❖ Painter's masking tape
- ❖ Drop cloths
- ❖ Paint roller and tray
- ❖ Flat latex paint for base coat
- ❖ Rubber gloves

- ❖ Lint-free, loosely knit, cotton cloth, such as jersey, cut into 18" (46 cm) squares
- ❖ Dark flat latex paint for top coat
- ❖ Light flat latex paint for top coat

1 Prepare the walls for painting (page 123). Protect the area around the walls with painter's masking tape and drop cloths (page 126). Apply the base coat and let it dry completely.

2 Put on rubber gloves. Scrunch up a piece of cloth and dip it into the dark paint. Squeeze out the excess paint. Beginning in an upper corner, dab the cloth over the wall surface in a 2-ft. (0.6 m) square area. Continue dabbing over the area, lifting any excess paint and reapplying it until the cloth is nearly dry. Allow some of the base coat to show through.

3 Use a clean piece of scrunched cloth to apply the light paint in the same manner. Allow some of the base coat and first overlay color to show through.

4 Repeat steps 2 and 3 in adjacent wall sections, blending areas together, until the entire wall is finished. Switch to clean cloths when they become saturated. Allow the wall to dry completely.

5 Dab more base-coat color onto any areas that appear too dense. Build depth and texture by dabbing on more dark paint. Add highlights by dabbing on more light paint.

3 Sponging

POUNCING PAINT onto the wall with a natural sea sponge produces a pebbly, mottled finish with color depth that invites a closer look. Sponge painting has changed through the years, yet continues to be popular because it is so easy to master and works well with so many décor styles. Today sponging is subtle and blended, unlike the high contrast in color that was once popular.

Different sponged effects can be produced, depending on the color choices, the number of color layers, and the density of the sponging. Colors that are similar in tone to the base-coat color produce the most harmonious results.

Understated monochromatic looks can be achieved by sponging various shades of the same color over a neutral base coat. Rich depth and color interest develop when two or three analogous hues are used. In general, the more open the sponged design, the more casual the appearance.

Sponging is often combined with other paint techniques and design elements. It can be teamed with solid-color painted walls in a guest room or whitewashed wainscoting in a formal dining area. Sponged stripes on a guest bath wall or a sponged border in a nursery can be very effective.

MATERIALS AND TOOLS

- ❖ Painter's masking tape
- ❖ Drop cloths
- ❖ Paint roller and tray
- ❖ Flat or semigloss latex paint for base coat
- ❖ Flat latex paint for top coat
- ❖ Water
- ❖ Bucket of water
- ❖ Paint bucket and mixing tool
- ❖ Rubber gloves
- ❖ Large natural sea sponge
- ❖ Small natural sea sponge
- ❖ Small paintbrush

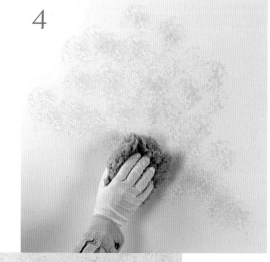

1 Prepare the walls for painting (page 123). Protect the area around the walls with painter's masking tape and drop cloths (page 126). Apply the base coat and let it dry completely.

2 Put on rubber gloves. In the bucket, prepare the glaze, mixing equal amounts of top-coat paint and water. Pour some of the paint mixture into the paint tray.

3 Soak the large sponge in water and squeeze tightly so the sponge is damp. Dip the sponge into the paint mixture and blot the excess onto the flat part of the tray.

4 Beginning at an upper corner, lightly pounce the sponge onto the wall in a 2-ft. (0.6 m) square area, getting as close as possible to the ceiling, corners, and moldings. Turn the sponge often to avoid repeating the pattern, and leave an irregular edge. Allow some of the base-coat color to show through.

5 Repeat step 4, moving down the wall to the bottom in a checkerboard pattern. Then go back to the top and fill in the open areas, blending into the irregular edges. Rinse the sponge often in warm water to keep it from clogging with paint. Squeeze out the sponge until it is only damp and start again.

6 Repeat steps 4 and 5 until each wall is covered. Use a small sea sponge or paintbrush to fill in corners and around moldings.

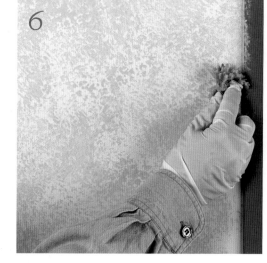

4 Ragging

RAGGING ENHANCES A WALL with a softly mottled layer of translucent color. In this technique, a crumpled rag saturated with glaze is pounced onto the wall. Although easy to master, ragging tends to be messy, so careful room preparation is important. Ragging is a good choice for hiding minor wall imperfections. It can be subtle enough for every wall in a room or applied to only one wall to create a focal point. Ragging can also be combined with a geometric technique, such as checks, stripes, or a harlequin design.

The colors selected for the base coat and glaze will influence the look and the style of décor for which it will be most suitable. Ragging is particularly attractive in cottage or country styled spaces with soft colors that clearly reveal the rag imprints. Two or three closely related colors can be ragged in layers. Values of the same color will have a quieter effect; contrasting colors will be more dramatic.

Any clean, lint-free rags can be used, including gauze, burlap, chamois cloth, or jersey. Woven cotton rags (used for the sample above) produce a blended look. Ragging can be applied sparsely, leaving much of the base color showing, or densely, creating a more solid appearance.

MATERIALS AND TOOLS

- ❖ Painter's masking tape
- ❖ Drop cloths
- ❖ Paint roller and tray
- ❖ Flat latex paint for base coat
- ❖ Paint bucket and mixing tool

- ❖ Latex paint for glaze mixture
- ❖ Water
- ❖ Water-based glazing liquid
- ❖ Rubber gloves

- ❖ Lint-free cotton rags, approximately 2 ft. (0.6 m) square
- ❖ Bucket of water
- ❖ Cardboard

3

4

5

1 Prepare the walls for painting (page 123). Protect the area around the walls with painter's masking tape and drop cloths (page 126). Apply the base coat and let it dry completely.

2 In the bucket, prepare the glaze, mixing equal amounts of paint, water, and glazing liquid to achieve a thin, creamy consistency.

3 Put on rubber gloves. Soak a rag in water and wring it out well. Dip the damp rag into the paint mixture and wring it out well. Draw the edges to the center and bunch the rag into random folds and creases.

4 Beginning in a top corner, pounce the rag randomly onto the wall, moving your entire arm in order to cover an area approximately 2 ft. (0.6 m) square. Work as close as possible to the ceiling, corners, and moldings. Leave irregular edges around the section. Reposition the rag in your hand to avoid repetitious patterns.

5 Repeat step 4 in another section, moving down the wall to the bottom in a checkerboard pattern. Then go back to the top and fill in the open areas, blending into the irregular edges. Reload the rag with paint as needed. When the cloth becomes slimy, rinse it in warm water, wring it out, and reload with paint, or begin with a clean rag.

6 Repeat steps 4 and 5 until each wall is covered.

7 To finish the room, hold a piece of cardboard against wall corners, ceiling, and moldings. Fill in gaps by dabbing lightly with a small piece of paint-filled cloth.

8 If additional colors are desired, allow the wall to dry completely before applying a second or third color.

5 Double Rolling

DOUBLE ROLLING allows even a beginner to apply an impressive decorative paint finish with minimal effort. Two paint colors are rolled onto the wall at once using a special roller that is split down the middle. As the roller moves back and forth through the paint, the colors mingle together, leaving a dramatic marbled effect that looks more complicated than it really is.

Colors that blend rather than contrast produce the most pleasing double-roller effects. For a monochromatic scheme, select two colors from one paint color card at least two or three value steps apart. Rolling colors that are close to

each other on the color wheel (like the orange and yellow-orange shown here) produces a more complex appearance with mottled patches of each paint color plus intermediate shades.

Double rollers fit onto standard 9" (23 cm) roller cages. Paint trays and tray liners with divided wells are also available. The double roller used in the photographs has a deep pile, which blends the colors with a soft, blurry texture. Double-roller covers with close-cropped sculpted shapes are also available. They blend colors in more distinct patterns.

MATERIALS AND TOOLS

- ❖ Painter's masking tape
- ❖ Drop cloths
- ❖ Paint roller and tray
- ❖ Latex paint for base coat
- ❖ Rubber gloves
- ❖ Latex paint for top coat in two colors
- ❖ Double roller with divided paint tray
- ❖ Small foam edging tool or paintbrush

1 Prepare the walls for painting (page 123). Protect the area around the walls with painter's masking tape and drop cloths (page 126). Apply the base coat and let it dry completely.

2 Put on rubber gloves. Pour the two paint colors into the divided paint tray. Dip the double roller into the paint. Each side of the roller will be loaded with a different paint color.

3 Beginning in a top corner, roll the paint over a 3-ft. (1 m) square section, moving the roller up and down and back and forth, covering the base coat and slightly blending the colors. Leave irregular edges. Reload the roller as necessary.

4 Repeat step 3 in adjacent areas from top to bottom and continuing around the room, blending along the irregular edges.

5 Load a small foam edging tool or paintbrush with both colors. Dab it onto the wall to blend both paint colors into corners and around woodwork.

6 Dragging/Strié

DRAGGING CREATES a patterned wall with fine, irregular streaks. It is also called strié, the French word for streak or groove. Dragging can be used to create a dignified, tailored background for paintings, antiques, and collections in a formal setting. With its sleek appearance, dragging also works well for contemporary spaces. For dining rooms with chair rails, dragging can be combined with plain painted or papered walls above or below the rail.

Dragging involves pulling a brush or similar tool vertically through wet paint glaze. You can use a wide paintbrush, wallpaper brush, steel wool, or a specialty strié brush; different tools create different patterns. The technique may take practice because it is important to keep the dragging strokes straight. The process tends to be messy, so prepare the room carefully. It is a good idea to work with someone—one person applies the glaze and the other drags.

Similar colors or different shades of one color will have a subtle effect. High-contrast colors create more apparent streaks. Pastels dragged over various shades of white or deeper colors dragged over a pastel base are popular choices for dragging. Deep jewel tones, such as emerald green or royal blue, are favorites for dragging in traditionally styled spaces.

- ❖ Painter's masking tape
- ❖ Drop cloths
- ❖ Paint roller and tray
- ❖ Satin latex paint for base coat
- ❖ Rubber gloves
- ❖ Paint bucket and mixing tool
- ❖ Latex paint for glaze mixture
- ❖ Water-based glazing liquid
- ❖ Wide, stiff, natural-bristle brush or other dragging tool
- ❖ Clean rags

1 Prepare the walls for painting (page 123). Protect the area around the walls with painter's masking tape and drop cloths (page 126). Apply the base coat and let it dry completely.

2 Put on rubber gloves. In the bucket, prepare the glaze, mixing one part latex paint with one part glazing liquid.

3 Apply the glaze from ceiling to floor in an 18" (46 cm) wide strip, using a roller. Make sure the wall surface is evenly covered.

4 While the glaze is still wet, lay the bristles flat against the surface and apply slight, even pressure on the back of the bristles as you pull the dragging tool downward through the glaze. Work from the ceiling to the baseboard in long, overlapping strokes.

5 Wipe off excess glaze from the brush onto rags after each downward stroke.

6 Repeat steps 3 to 5, moving around the room until all the walls are finished.

7 Color Weaving

COLOR WEAVING IS THREE layers of dragging (page 24) applied in alternating directions. Because each layer is a different color, the result is a rich, dimensional effect that resembles woven fabric. This technique is a budget-wise alternative to wallpapers or fabric wall treatments.

The dragging tools and colors selected will vary the look. Specialty dragging brushes are usually 2" to 3" (5 to 7.5 cm) wide, though regular paintbrushes are available in a wide variety of sizes and work just as well. Coarse weave brushes leave wider streaks, revealing more color and making the space appear more casual. Bright colors combined in a coarse weave work well for casual living spaces such as a family room. For the example above, a standard 4" (10 cm) paintbrush and warm colors with high value contrast were used, resulting in a casual, imperfect look. Fine weave brushes and a subtle color scheme produce a more sophisticated look. Monochromatic tones and a fine weave would be elegant in a formal dining room.

Although different color combinations may be used, three distinct values (light, medium, and dark) are recommended. It is always best to apply the dark value in the bottom layer, the light value in the middle, and the medium value on top.

MATERIALS AND TOOLS

- ❖ Painter's masking tape
- ❖ Drop cloths
- ❖ Three paint rollers and tray with liners
- ❖ Light color latex paint for base coat
- ❖ Rubber gloves
- ❖ Paint bucket and mixing tool
- ❖ Water-based glazing liquid
- ❖ Latex paint in three colors for glaze mixtures
- ❖ Paintbrush, 4" (10 cm) wide
- ❖ Clean rags

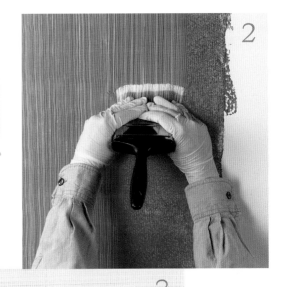

1 Prepare the walls for painting (page 123). Protect the area around the walls with painter's masking tape and drop cloths (page 126). Apply the base coat and let it dry completely.

2 Put on rubber gloves. Mix the first glaze, following manufacturer's instructions. Apply the glaze to the wall and drag through it *vertically*, following the steps for dragging on page 25. Let the wall dry completely.

3 Mix the second glaze. Apply the glaze to the wall and drag through it *horizontally*, following the steps for dragging. Let the wall dry completely.

4 Mix the third glaze slightly thinner than the first two. Apply the glaze to the wall and drag through it *vertically*, following the steps for dragging. Let the wall dry completely. The thinner glaze will allow more of the first two colors to show through.

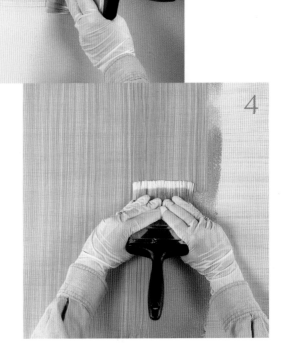

8 Combing

COMBING COVERS A WALL with narrow, distinct lines by drawing a comb through wet glaze to reveal the base coat. The technique is fairly simple but requires a steady hand to produce an even, straight pattern. Working with a partner creates more consistent results; one person applies the glaze, and the other combs through it. The technique works best on smooth walls where the combing tool won't skip.

Depending upon the comb, colors, and pattern used, combing can appear delicate or bold. Painting combs and rubber squeegees with notches cut into them are the most common combing tools. Walls can be combed horizontally or vertically. Combed pinstripes in upscale earthy browns are attractive in formal spaces. Soft pastels with low contrast can be used to comb an entire wall or room, creating a soothing, relaxed atmosphere. Vertical combing under a chair rail mimics wainscoting. Combing can also be done in patterns, such as zigzags, swirls, or wavy lines. This effect, however, can be distracting, so it's best to use such designs in small spaces. Molding-framed wall areas can be attractively emphasized with subtle-colored combed swirls. Vibrant combed hues in a contemporary design above a fireplace or wet bar serve as a dramatic focal point that enlivens the entire space.

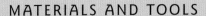

- ❖ Painter's masking tape
- ❖ Drop cloths
- ❖ Paint roller and tray
- ❖ Latex paint for base coat
- ❖ Rubber gloves
- ❖ Paint bucket and mixing tool
- ❖ Latex paint for glaze mixture
- ❖ Water-based glazing liquid
- ❖ Combing tool of choice
- ❖ Clean rags

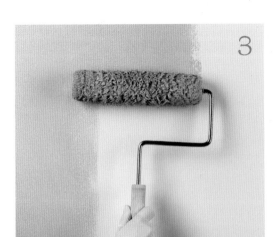

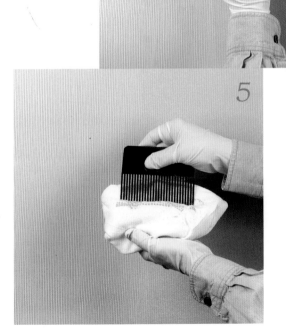

1 Prepare the walls for painting (page 123). Protect the area around the walls with painter's masking tape and drop cloths (page 126). Apply the base coat and let it dry completely.

2 Put on rubber gloves. In the bucket, prepare the glaze, mixing one part latex paint with two parts glazing liquid.

3 Apply the glaze from ceiling to floor in a 2-ft. (0.6 m) wide strip, using a roller. Make sure the wall surface is evenly covered.

4 While the glaze is still wet, pull the combing tool downward through the glaze from the ceiling to the baseboard, applying even, relaxed pressure. The teeth of the combing tool remove lines of glaze, allowing the base coat to show through.

5 Wipe off excess glaze from the combing tool onto rags after each downward stroke.

6 Repeat steps 3 to 5, moving around the room until all the walls are finished.

9 Feathering

A SIMPLE WAY to produce a custom look, feathering is a technique that even the beginning painter can master. Contrasting paint is lightly pounced onto the wall, using an ordinary feather duster. Feathering doesn't require patience or a steady hand, and the tools are inexpensive. As easy as the technique may be, however, it is always a good idea to practice on a large piece of tagboard before applying the paint to the wall.

Purchase several feather dusters made from long wing feathers, rather than short, fluffy breast and back feathers. They cost less because they don't dust as well, but they produce better results for this technique.

Feathering with white or off-white paint can be used to tone down an intense base coat. Colorful, rich, and creamy shades feathered over walls of the same color in a lighter or darker value create a dreamy appearance for walls in a nursery or a young child's bedroom and bathroom. Feathering can also be applied in wide vertical stripes or as a high border.

- ❖ Painter's masking tape
- ❖ Drop cloths
- ❖ Paint roller and tray
- ❖ Latex paint for base coat
- ❖ Rubber gloves
- ❖ Several feather dusters
- ❖ Newspaper
- ❖ Latex paint for top coat, same sheen as base coat

1 Prepare the walls for painting (page 123). Protect the area around the walls with painter's masking tape and drop cloths (page 126). Apply the base coat and let it dry completely.

2 Put on rubber gloves. Gently dab the end of a feather duster into the top-coat paint and lightly tap off the excess paint onto newspaper.

3 Beginning at a top corner and working out and down, gently pounce the feather duster onto the wall. Turn the duster often to vary the pattern. Reload the duster with paint as necessary. Leave irregular edges.

4 Continue around the room, always working back into the irregular edges. Stand back from the wall often to check for a consistently dense feathering pattern. If the feathers become clogged with paint and the design becomes too heavy, simply switch to a new duster.

10 Whisking

WHISKING DRESSES A WALL with curved streaks. It is similar to dragging (page 24), though the tool used to pattern the wall is a whisk broom, drawn through top-coat paint in short swirls. The technique is easy and inexpensive. Buy a new whisk broom and count on throwing it away when you finish painting the wall.

In addition to the swirled pattern shown here, other whisking options include pulling the whisk broom vertically through the paint, free-form crisscrossing curves, and wavy lines. When whisking, it is important to apply enough pressure to leave string-like stripes. Whenever possible, complete an entire wall without stopping to achieve a uniform look.

For the most effective results, select colors with high contrast for the base coat and top coat. The top coat will be the most apparent color. Use satin or semigloss paint for the base coat so the broom bristles can easily sweep off some of the top coat. Whisked walls can be quite "busy," so it is best to use this technique for small wall spaces, such as below a chair rail or as a border.

MATERIALS AND TOOLS

- ❖ Painter's masking tape
- ❖ Drop cloths
- ❖ Paint roller and tray
- ❖ Satin or semigloss latex paint for base coat
- ❖ Rubber gloves
- ❖ Satin latex paint for top coat
- ❖ Whisk broom
- ❖ Paper towels or clean rags

1 Prepare the walls for painting (page 123). Protect the area around the walls with painter's masking tape and drop cloths (page 126). Apply the base coat and let it dry completely.

2 Put on rubber gloves. Starting at the upper corner, roll on a single, 2-ft. (0.6 m) wide, vertical stripe of paint with the paint roller.

3 Sweep the whisk broom through the wet paint in overlapping swirling motions. Keep a narrow wet edge unwhisked.

4 Repeat steps 2 and 3 immediately alongside the first whisked stripe, working back into the wet edge. Use paper towels or clean rags to clean the bristles as needed. Continue across the wall without stopping in order to whisk the entire surface while the paint is wet.

11 Troweling

TROWELING LAYERS PAINT on the wall with a hand trowel. Dark, medium, and light color values applied to the wall this way produce a dramatically textured, weathered appearance. This method provides only the illusion of texture, leaving the wall very smooth, so the wall can be easily repainted at a future date. Troweling works best on flat, uninterrupted walls where it is easy to manipulate the trowel. No base coat is necessary and the technique is extremely forgiving, making this an easy finish.

The randomness of the application and the wide range of color choices will make the results unique. Although troweling requires at least three color values, more colors can be added if desired. To achieve powerful color effects, use deep earth tones or striking jewel tones. Paler hues, such as soft pastels or various tinted whites combined with neutral tones, produce more muted effects.

Concentrating darker colors in the corners and along the baseboard lends an overall timeworn look to the wall, perfect for aging a vintage styled kitchen in a new home. A combination of deep mustard, golden honey, rich sand, and slate tones would tone down a sun-drenched breakfast room to create a more soothing dining area.

- ❖ Painter's masking tape
- ❖ Drop cloths
- ❖ Rubber gloves
- ❖ Semigloss latex paint in three color values
- ❖ Large aluminum foil roasting pan
- ❖ Small plastic trowel
- ❖ Clean rags

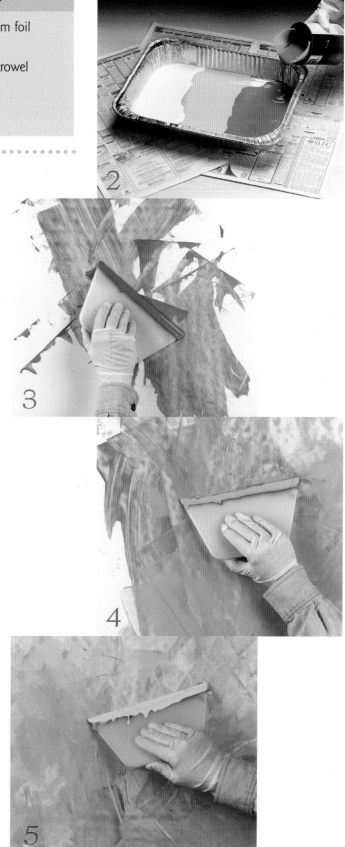

1 Prepare the walls for painting (page 123). Protect the area around the walls with painter's masking tape and drop cloths (page 126).

2 Put on rubber gloves. Pour the three paints into the foil pan, with the dark value on one side, the medium value in the center, and the light value on the other side. Add more of each color until the paint is at least 2" (5 cm) deep.

3 Dip the trowel about 1" (2.5 cm) deep into the dark paint. Beginning in an upper corner of the wall, apply the paint by wiping it from the trowel in short strokes in random directions. Repeat to cover an area about 3 ft. (1 m) square. Much of the bare wall will show through.

4 Repeat step 3 with the medium paint, applying it in areas not covered by the dark paint. It is not necessary to clean the trowel, as it is desirable to have the colors mix together slightly.

5 Repeat step 3 with the light paint, building depth and texture.

6 Apply more of each paint value as desired, blending them slightly and creating a rough plaster look. Clean the trowel as necessary with clean rags.

7 Repeat steps 3 to 6 in adjacent areas, moving down and across the entire wall. Stand back and look at the wall occasionally. Go back and add more paint to areas that need highlights or shadows.

12 Paper Frottage

PAPER APPLIED OVER WET GLAZE and then removed will absorb some of the glaze and leave a distinctive imprint on the wall. This technique, called paper frottage, gives unique depth and color variation to the wall. It can be used alone or as a stylish background for other applications, such as stencils, freehand designs, or even murals.

In the example above, ordinary copy-machine paper was applied to the glaze and removed in rows, producing a finish that resembles stone blocks. Variations of the paper frottage theme can be achieved by using different kinds of paper. Lining paper, tissue paper, corrugated paper, craft paper, newspaper, or paper shopping bags can be used; each produces a distinctive look. You can also overlap papers at random angles or lightly crumple and manipulate the paper before applying it to the glaze.

Using two different intensities of one color for the base coat and glaze results in a subtle appearance. Bolder effects happen with two highly contrasting colors. The paper will absorb a lot of the glaze and leave a sheer veil of glaze color over the base coat with patches of concentrated color.

- Painter's masking tape
- Drop cloths
- Paint roller and tray
- Latex paint for base coat
- Rubber gloves
- Paint bucket and mixing tool
- Latex paint for top coat
- Flat water-based glazing liquid
- Paper (8½" × 11" or larger)

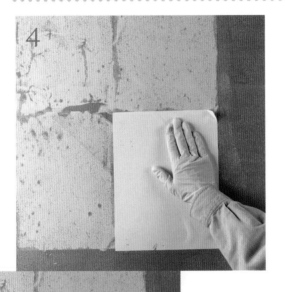

1 Prepare the walls for painting (page 123). Protect the area around the walls with painter's masking tape and drop cloths (page 126). Apply the base coat and let it dry completely.

2 Put on rubber gloves. In the bucket, prepare the glaze, mixing one part paint with one part glazing liquid.

3 Beginning at the top of the wall and working downward, apply glaze to the wall in a 4-ft. (1.2 m) square section using the paint roller.

4 Fold up one corner of the paper so it will be easier to remove. Press the paper directly into the wet glaze.

5 Peel the paper from the wall by carefully pulling the folded corner.

6 Repeat steps 4 and 5 throughout the glazed area, leaving a narrow wet edge of glaze. Align sheets of paper in rows as shown or overlap papers at various angles for a less distinct pattern.

7 Repeat steps 3 to 6 until the entire wall is complete.

13 Bubble Wrap

THIS DECORATIVE PAINT technique produces a pebbled imprint of little "bubbles" all over the wall. Glaze is applied to the wall and manipulated with common plastic bubble wrap that has been secured to a rubber grout float for easy handling. This process is fun, but it can get a bit messy, so prepare the room well and have lots of clean rags handy.

Any compact area that could use a healthy dose of pattern and color is a good candidate for the bubble wrap technique. Cool pastel colors, such as muted blue, pale green, soft aqua, and gentle turquoise, result in soothing, lighthearted effects. Applying bubbles onto a half-wall in a nursery using soft pastel tones creates a subtle pattern for the space. Bubbles are a festive way to add a border of bright, primary colors in a children's bathroom. Stripes of bubbles in a bright, sunny color scheme could liven up a laundry room. Using a deep-toned metallic paint color, the pebbled pattern would be a dramatic effect for a backsplash wall behind a wet bar in a family room.

MATERIALS AND TOOLS

- ❖ Painter's masking tape
- ❖ Drop cloths
- ❖ Paint roller and tray
- ❖ Satin latex paint for base coat
- ❖ Rubber gloves
- ❖ Bubble wrap
- ❖ Rubber grout float
- ❖ Semigloss latex paint for glaze mixture
- ❖ Semigloss water-based glazing liquid
- ❖ Paint bucket and mixing tool
- ❖ Clean rags

1 Prepare the walls for painting (page 123). Protect the area around the walls with painter's masking tape and drop cloths (page 126). Apply the base coat and let it dry completely.

2 Cover the bottom and sides of the rubber float with bubble wrap. Secure the edges with masking tape.

3 Put on rubber gloves. In the bucket, prepare the glaze, mixing one part latex paint with one part glazing liquid.

4 Apply the glaze from ceiling to floor in a 18" (46 cm) wide strip, using a roller. Make sure the wall surface is evenly covered.

5 Beginning in an upper corner, press the bubble wrap into the glaze and lift it straight back. Repeat several times, turning the float at different angles, creating bubble impressions. Wipe excess glaze from the bubble wrap onto clean rags as necessary. Continue until the entire strip is bubbled. Leave a wet edge.

6 Apply another strip of glaze next to the first one and repeat step 5, blending the bubble impressions back into the first area. Continue until the entire wall is bubbled. Rewrap the float with fresh bubble wrap as necessary.

14 Stippling

STIPPLING COVERS THE WALL with fine, pinpoint dots that produce a delicate texture. The finish is most effective on walls that are in good condition, as the glaze can accentuate surface imperfections.

Unless you are stippling only a small area, use a two-person team to speed up the process. The first partner applies the vertical strips of glaze and the other stipples the glaze. It is a good idea to wipe the stippling brush frequently to be sure the glaze is manipulated, not removed. Work continuously and quickly for even results.

The stippling technique works with many colors. Though translucent, the glaze color will be dominant, as most of it will remain on the wall. Light tones and pastel-colored base coats will soften and lighten a dark or bold glaze color. Stippling a light glaze over a bright jewel tone mellows the base-coat color considerably, but allows bright color to peek through.

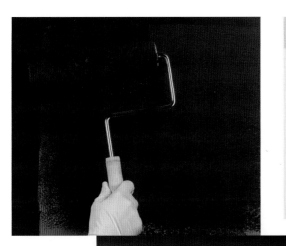

MATERIALS AND TOOLS

- ❖ Painter's masking tape
- ❖ Drop cloths
- ❖ Paint roller and tray
- ❖ Rubber gloves
- ❖ Latex paint for base coat
- ❖ Paint bucket and mixing tool

- ❖ Latex paint for top coat
- ❖ Water-based glazing liquid
- ❖ Paintbrush, 2" (5 cm) wide
- ❖ Foam applicator, 2" (5 cm) wide
- ❖ Block stippler
- ❖ Edge stippler or stencil brush

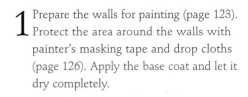

1 Prepare the walls for painting (page 123). Protect the area around the walls with painter's masking tape and drop cloths (page 126). Apply the base coat and let it dry completely.

2 Put on rubber gloves. In the bucket, prepare the glaze, mixing equal amounts of top-coat paint and glazing liquid. Pour some of the mixture into the well of the paint tray.

3 Beginning in an upper corner, apply the glaze mixture to the wall in a 2-ft. (0.6 m) vertical strip. Use a 2" (5 cm) paintbrush to cut in along the ceiling and wall corner; use the paint roller to fill in the wall.

4 Apply a small amount of the glaze mixture to the block stippler, using a foam applicator, to ensure that the first pounce will not remove an excessive amount of glaze. This is called "buttering" the stippler.

5 Stipple the wall with a pouncing action. Move your arm in a circular motion, overlapping the imprints as you work from the top of the wall to the bottom. Leave an unstippled wet edge where the adjacent strip will be applied.

6 Repeat steps 3 to 5 until the entire wall is complete. Use a small edge stippler or stencil brush to stipple the corners and around woodwork.

15 Spattering

FLICKING SMALL DOTS of different colored paint haphazardly onto a wall results in a speckled, casual wall. The colors selected for spattering and the density that each color is spattered determine the look. Spattering is often used effectively in country styled interiors. Picture a vintage farmhouse kitchen with spattered walls that serve as a backdrop to black, white, and red collections and antiques.

Although easy to master, the process can be messy. Use a stiff, short-bristled brush to load the paint and a paint stirring stick or wooden craft stick to cause the spatters. Test the technique against a sheet of tagboard before you begin. If some of the dots drip, add more paint to the glaze mixture.

Apply the spatters sparsely at first, as an area can always be spattered again. If more than one color of dots is being applied, spatter the first round sparsely and then go back and add colors.

The base coat will remain the dominant color. When colors are spattered on a light-colored base coat, the effect is much lighter and airier than when the same colors are spattered on a darker base-coat color.

MATERIALS AND TOOLS

- ❖ Painter's masking tape
- ❖ Drop cloths
- ❖ Paint roller and tray
- ❖ Satin latex paint for base coat
- ❖ Rubber gloves
- ❖ Paint bucket and mixing tool
- ❖ Satin latex paint for spattering
- ❖ Water-based glazing liquid
- ❖ Stiff paintbrush, 3" (7.5 cm) wide
- ❖ Spatter stick

1 Prepare the walls for painting (page 123). Protect the area around the walls with painter's masking tape and drop cloths (page 126). Apply the base coat and let it dry completely.

2 Put on rubber gloves. In the bucket, prepare the glaze, mixing two parts paint, two parts glazing liquid, and one part water. It should be the consistency of heavy cream.

3 Dip the brush about 1/2" (1.3 cm) into the glaze mixture. Remove excess paint. Hold the brush upright with the bristles perpendicular to the wall. Holding the spatter stick parallel to the wall, pull it toward you across the tips of the bristles, releasing a spray of paint flecks onto the wall. Begin in an upper corner and work outward and down, directing the spatters by turning the brush slightly. Reload the brush when the spatters get too fine.

4 Repeat step 3 until the walls are complete. Repeat with a second color of glaze mix, if desired.

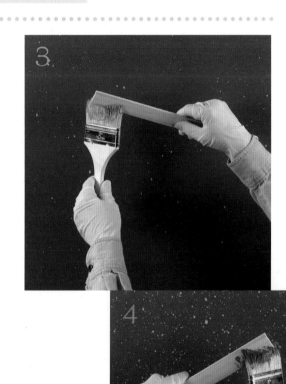

Geometric DESIGNS

Repetitive linear patterns and shapes can be painted on walls to create many effects, from bold and playful to subtle and sophisticated. The nine geometric designs in this section can be used to paint focal areas, borders, wainscoting, or entire rooms.

_16_ Stripes

VERSATILE AND APPEALING, stripes can be part of many décors. Stripes provide an eye-catching backdrop for a gallery of artwork. They can visually expand a small foyer or perk up a boring hallway or landing. In a kitchen, stripes can be an innovative treatment above upper cabinets. Wide stripes can relax formal furnishings in a living room.

There are lots of color choices for stripes. Colors with high contrast produce a dramatic effect that can be used for showcasing contemporary spaces. Pinstripes in rich colors look formal. Stimulating, vivid stripes are often found in children's play areas. Exciting inspiration for striped designs can be found in clothing and home décor fabrics. Stripes are also combined with other paint techniques such as sponging, ragging, or combing.

The success of a striped design depends on accurate measuring and taping. Though shown with a carpenter's level, a laser level will make the technique easier. When choosing the width of the stripes, consider the size of the wall as well as the time you want to dedicate to the project. Traditional stripes are 3" to 5" (7.5 to 12.7 cm) wide. The spaces between the stripes can be wider, narrower, or equal to the stripes. Spaces the same width as painter's tape can be taped off quickly.

MATERIALS AND TOOLS

- ❖ Painter's masking tape
- ❖ Drop cloths
- ❖ Paint roller and tray
- ❖ Latex paint for base coat
- ❖ Pencil
- ❖ Carpenter's or laser level

- ❖ Ruler
- ❖ Small plastic smoothing tool
- ❖ Rubber gloves
- ❖ Latex paint for top coat
- ❖ Small roller or paintbrush
- ❖ Artist's paintbrush

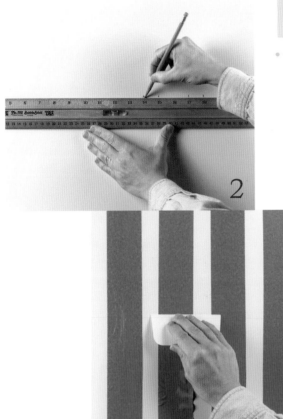

1 Prepare the walls for painting (page 123). Protect the area around the walls with painter's masking tape and drop cloths (page 126). Apply the base coat and let it dry completely.

2 For even stripes, use the carpenter's level to mark a series of tick marks from floor to ceiling at the center of the wall. Mark a line of tick marks on each side of the first line a distance away equal to half the desired width of the stripes. These lines indicate your center stripe. For uneven stripes, measure the width of the first stripe from one corner of the wall; mark a series of tick marks from floor to ceiling.

3 Continue marking the measurements to indicate subsequent stripes. When you reach a corner, either adjust the stripe widths to end exactly in the corner or keep constant widths and wrap a stripe around the corner.

4 Apply painter's masking tape to mask the areas between stripes. Smooth down the edge of the tape along the marked lines, using a small plastic smoothing tool. This prevents the paint from seeping under the tape, producing an imperfect edge.

5 Put on rubber gloves. Apply a top-coat paint to the exposed areas using a small roller or paintbrush.

6 Carefully remove the masking tape before the paint dries. If there has been any seepage under the tape, touch it up with a small artist's paintbrush.

17 Sheen Stripes

SHEEN STRIPING is a simple and subtle way to add interest to the wall without expanding the existing color palette. Glossy stripes are painted over a flat background of the same color, creating an elegant contrast that is particularly suitable for formal spaces. Consider using sheen striping in a room that holds treasured antiques or traditionally styled furnishings.

Variations in the width of the stripes add visual interest and distinctiveness to the striped design. You can alternate extra-wide stripes with very narrow stripes or gradually increase the width of the stripes at regular intervals from narrow to wide. Apply the glossy stripes to one focus wall or to all the walls in the room.

Color options for sheen stripes are directly related to the existing color scheme in the room. The effect is more pronounced, however, with deep colors, such as the brilliant blue shown above, rich burgundy, or emerald green. Light, muted sheen stripes work well in smaller spaces, rooms that contain low ceilings, and areas that lack natural lighting. Deeper, richer sheen stripes add warmth and coziness to oversized rooms and open-concept homes with high ceilings.

- ❖ Painter's masking tape
- ❖ Drop cloths
- ❖ Paint roller and tray
- ❖ Flat latex paint for base coat
- ❖ Pencil
- ❖ Carpenter's or laser level
- ❖ Small plastic smoothing tool
- ❖ Water-based glazing liquid
- ❖ Rubber gloves
- ❖ Small paintbrush
- ❖ Semigloss latex paint for top coat in same color as base coat

1 Prepare the walls for painting (page 123). Protect the area around the walls with painter's masking tape and drop cloths (page 126). Apply the flat base coat and let it dry completely.

2 Mark and mask off stripes, as in steps 2 to 4 on page 47.

3 Put on rubber gloves. Apply glazing liquid along the inside edges of the tape, using the small paintbrush. Allow to dry completely. This will ensure crisp, straight edges by preventing the paint from seeping under the tape.

4 Paint the stripes, using the semigloss paint. Remove the tape. Allow to dry completely.

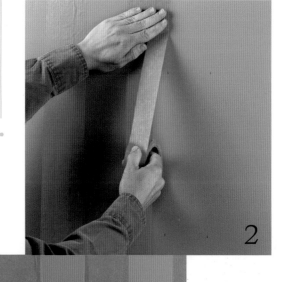

18 Checks

CLASSIC CHECKS consist of squares painted in a repeating, alternating pattern over a background color. They can be a stylish accent in a casual styled kitchen, either under a chair rail or as a border around the room. Bright colored checks are playful and charming in a child's bedroom. So the strong pattern does not overwhelm the area, take color and scale into consideration. You can apply surprisingly oversized checks to one wall in a room.

For the most effective checked design, choose a light background color and paint the checks in a medium or dark value color. This is especially important if complementary colors are used, so the colors will not fight for dominance. Colors that are close to each other on the color wheel, such as blue and green, produce handsome combinations. Along with solid colors, decorative paint techniques, such as sponging (page 18), can be used.

Though it may take a lot of time, careful masking of the checks is crucial to the success of this application. A laser level will make the job faster and easier.

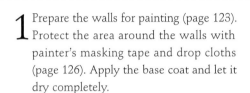

MATERIALS AND TOOLS

- ❖ Painter's masking tape
- ❖ Drop cloths
- ❖ Paint roller and tray
- ❖ Latex paint for base coat
- ❖ Tape measure
- ❖ Pencil
- ❖ Carpenter's or laser level
- ❖ Putty knife
- ❖ Latex paint for top coat
- ❖ Paintbrush or small roller

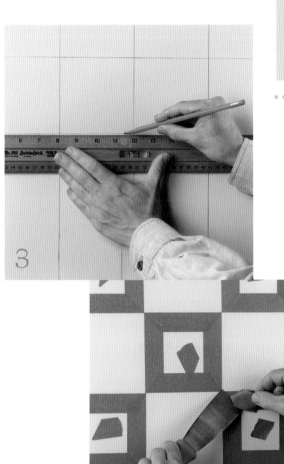

1 Prepare the walls for painting (page 123). Protect the area around the walls with painter's masking tape and drop cloths (page 126). Apply the base coat and let it dry completely.

2 Measure the height and width of the wall to be painted. Decide on the scale of your check. If the wall cannot be divided evenly, begin the design at the ceiling, allowing it to run out at the floor, where smaller squares will be less obvious.

3 Mark a series of tick marks from floor to ceiling for the sides of the first row of squares. Use a carpenter's level to ensure the line is plumb. Join the marks, using a pencil. Repeat to mark all the vertical lines. Then mark the horizontal lines, measuring evenly from the baseboard.

4 Apply painter's masking tape to mask off the squares that will remain the base-coat color; use a putty knife to trim masking tape diagonally at the corners, as shown. Smooth down the tape edges to prevent seepage. Mark the inside of each square not being painted at this time with a piece of tape.

5 Paint the remaining squares, using a paintbrush or small roller. Carefully remove the tape. Allow the paint to dry. Touch up any areas where paint may have seeped under the tape.

19 Color Blocking

SQUARES AND RECTANGLES painted in various sizes and colors are a fresh, dramatic look, especially suitable for contemporary spaces. Large, oversized blocks make the most effective design statement. Due to the large scale of the blocks, quantity of blocks, and number of colors used, the technique is most effective when painted on only one wall in a room.

It is not uncommon for blocks of color to take the place of artwork on the wall. Consider using the technique above a whirlpool in a master bathroom, behind a sofa in a family room, or above a sideboard in a dining room.

Choose a family of colors in tasteful, muted shades and paint them in one-yard blocks or larger to create a striking wall treatment. For a small focus area, slightly brighter hues in 12" to 18" (30.5 to 46 cm) blocks will produce a bolder overall look. Soothing monochromatic effects can be achieved by using varying intensities of the same color.

MATERIALS AND TOOLS

- Painter's masking tape
- Drop cloths
- Paint roller and tray
- Two or more shades of satin latex paint
- Colored pencils to match paints
- Carpenter's or laser level
- Foam applicator
- Water-based glazing liquid

1 Prepare the walls for painting (page 123). Protect the area around the walls with painter's masking tape and drop cloths (page 126). Apply the base coat in the lightest color and let it dry completely.

2 Map out the block design on the wall, using a carpenter's level or laser level and the colored pencils that coordinate with each paint color.

3 Apply painter's masking tape around the blocks that will be painted with the first color, aligning the tape to the outer edges of the colored pencil lines.

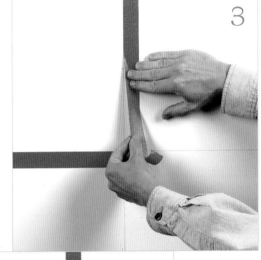

4 Apply glazing liquid along the inside edge of the tape, using a foam applicator. Let the glaze dry completely. This will ensure crisp, straight edges by preventing the paint from seeping under the tape.

5 Paint the first set of blocks in the desired color, using the small roller. Carefully remove the tape while the paint is still wet. Let the paint dry completely.

6 Repeat steps 3 to 5 for the blocks in each paint color.

20 Diamond Border

THE DIAMOND BORDER is a simple pattern with timeless appeal. Tailored, formal settings can be accented with traditional black and white diamonds. Bright-colored diamond borders are a cheerful motif in children's rooms. Subtle looks can be achieved by painting the diamonds in two shades from the same paint color card or by choosing the same color and alternating the paint sheens.

Scale the size of the diamond border to suit the size of the wall and the room. Consider the colors of the fabrics and furnishings in the room when choosing the diamond colors. Popular

large-scale diamonds have a greater impact when the furnishings are sleek and simple. Blend the décor of adjoining rooms by extending the diamond border from one room onto one wall of the next room. Unify an open-concept living space by painting sections of the diamond border in several areas.

There are many creative ways to personalize a diamond border. The diamonds can be color washed (page 14), sponge painted (page 18), ragged (page 20), or combed (page 28). Applying upholstery tacks or beads at the points where the diamonds intersect gives a distinctive touch to the border.

MATERIALS AND TOOLS

- ❖ Painter's masking tape
- ❖ Drop cloths
- ❖ Paint roller and tray
- ❖ Latex paint for base coat
- ❖ Pencil
- ❖ Tape measure
- ❖ Carpenter's or laser level
- ❖ Cardboard for template
- ❖ Latex paint for top coat in two colors
- ❖ Small roller or paintbrush

3

1 Prepare the walls for painting (page 123). Protect the area around the walls with painter's masking tape and drop cloths (page 126). Apply the base coat and let it dry completely. Using a carpenter's level or laser level and tape measure, mark a faint horizontal pencil line on the wall at the desired center line of the border.

2 Measure the width of the wall space to be covered. Divide by the approximate desired diamond width, and round up to the nearest whole number to determine the number of diamonds. Then divide the space measurement by the number of diamonds to determine the exact diamond width. Make a cardboard diamond template with this width and the desired height. Draw a line across the center.

4

3 Match up the line on the template to the line on the wall, and trace the diamonds along the border with a pencil.

4 Apply masking tape to the outside of every other diamond, overlapping the tape at each corner of the diamond.

5 Apply the first top-coat color inside the taped-off diamonds, using the small roller.

6 Remove the tape while paint is still wet. Allow the paint to dry completely.

7 Repeat steps 4 to 6 with the second color to paint the remaining diamonds.

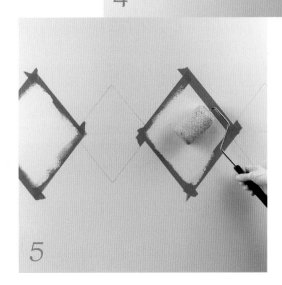

5

21 Lattice

THIS LATTICE FINISH is a freehand glaze manipulation technique that results in a sheer diagonal grid. The Color Shaper tool used to create the lattice is shaped like a paintbrush but has a solid, flat, rubber end instead of bristles. It is available from specialty paint stores or art supply centers. A small putty knife could also be used.

White or off-white glaze applied over a medium or dark base-coat color will give the most realistic appearance. Bright, vivid base-coat colors can liven up an art studio or craft area. Soft pastel colors may enhance a child's bedroom. Washed, earthy tones look natural in a sunroom or behind a potting bench.

Lattice works well as a companion to other techniques. Painted on the bottom half of the wall in dining area, the lattice technique resembles wainscoting. A stenciled or freehand painted climbing vine can be applied over the lattice design as part of a botanical themed bathroom. Alongside stairs, the lattice design forms an interesting backdrop where family portraits can be hung.

MATERIALS AND TOOLS

- ❖ Painter's masking tape
- ❖ Drop cloths
- ❖ Paint roller and tray
- ❖ Semigloss latex paint for base coat
- ❖ Rubber gloves
- ❖ Paint bucket and mixing tool
- ❖ Water-based glazing liquid
- ❖ Latex paint in desired glaze color
- ❖ Soft-bristle paintbrush
- ❖ Flat Color Shaper, 2" (5 cm) wide
- ❖ Clean rags

1 Prepare the walls for painting (page 123). Protect the area around the walls with painter's masking tape and drop cloths (page 126). Apply the base coat and let it dry completely.

2 Put on rubber gloves. In the bucket, prepare the glaze, mixing three parts glazing liquid with one part paint. Using the paintbrush, apply the glaze mixture evenly over the wall surface.

3 While the wall is wet, draw the Color Shaper through the glaze in freehand diagonal stripes. After each stripe, wipe excess paint from the tool onto clean rags.

4 Repeat step 3 in the opposite direction, creating a lattice effect.

22 Plaid

IN THIS PLAID design, horizontal and vertical stripes of alternating colors and widths are applied freehand, resulting in a casual, wonderfully imperfect appearance. The multicolor plaid design is most effective and easiest to paint where there are no windows, doors, or other interruptions in the wall surface.

Two-color blended lines are achieved by "double loading" the paintbrush. It is critical to always load and hold the brush in the same position to avoid reversing the paint colors. Pouring only a small amount of paint at a time into shallow containers helps prevent the paint colors from mixing together. If an entire stripe

cannot be completed with one stroke, it is better to begin the next stroke from the opposite direction, painting it back into the first stroke. This results in a more continuous joining of colors and a more harmonious look. Chalk guidelines help space the strokes evenly.

Size and scale are important. Small rooms are prime candidates for smaller scale plaids in light or neutral colors. If there are other strong design elements in the room, consider painting the plaid on only one wall or half-wall. A bold hue that is part of the existing color scheme can be accentuated by bringing that color into the plaid design.

1 Prepare the walls for painting (page 123). Protect the area around the walls with painter's masking tape and drop cloths (page 126). Apply the base coat and let it dry completely.

2 Mark the plaid pattern on the wall with tick marks, using a pencil. Use chalk to sketch out the plaid pattern on the wall.

3 Pour small amounts of the first two colors into shallow containers. Dip the foam applicator into one color; gently tap the back of the applicator against the container rim to remove excess paint. Next, dip one edge of the applicator into the second color of paint. This method of adding paint to the applicator is called "double loading."

4 Paint the first vertical stripe of the plaid, beginning at the top of the wall and pulling the applicator downward until the paint gets too thin.

5 Double load the applicator again and complete the stripe, painting back into the first stroke to blend the strokes together.

6 Repeat steps 4 and 5 until all the vertical stripes have been painted. Allow the vertical stripes to dry for two hours.

7 Repeat steps 3 to 6 for the horizontal stripes.

23 : Polka Dots

A LIVELY, LIGHTHEARTED paint technique, polka dots are often inspired by a fun dotted fabric. This playful effect is perfect for children's rooms, craft rooms, laundry rooms, bathrooms, and more. Part of the success of this technique depends on adjusting the spacing of the polka dots to suit the size of the room. Do not worry if the polka dots are imperfect, as randomness is part of what makes this technique special.

Choice of color depends mostly on where the polka dots are used. Consider brighter colors for lively spaces like children's playrooms, bedrooms, and bathrooms. If you select complementary colors, as shown above, use a lighter value for the background color so the dots pop. Use subdued colors, perhaps two shades of the same color, for a guest bedroom or guest bathroom where the goal is to create a one-of-a-kind look. Color washing (page 14) the walls before applying polka dots will soften the look. For a reversible scheme, choose colors for the background and dots on one wall and reverse the colors on an adjacent wall.

1 Prepare the walls for painting (page 123). Protect the area around the walls with painter's masking tape and drop cloths (page 126). Apply the base coat and let it dry completely.

2 Plan the spacing of the polka dots. Place small pieces of masking tape wherever you would like the dots placed.

3 Pour a puddle of paint onto a paper plate. Dip the open end of a Styrofoam cup into the puddle and dab lightly onto several paper towels to remove excess paint.

4 Press the cup firmly over the tape mark on the wall. Repeat to outline each polka dot.

5 Using a small foam applicator, fill in each polka dot with its paint color.

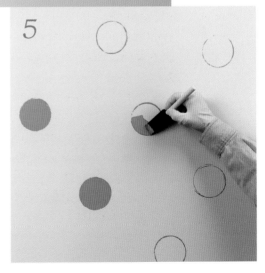

24 | Basket Weave

THE BASKET WEAVE technique is a variation of combing (page 28), worked with a triangular graining tool. The sides of the graining tool are rubber combs with teeth of different widths and spacing. The repeated dragging, lifting, and repositioning of the tool in the wet glaze results in a fluid, imperfect design resembling woven wicker.

A somewhat time-consuming process with effective but busy results, the basket weave technique is best used in small, casual areas such as a laundry room or mudroom or on the wall space between kitchen cabinets and the countertop. The basket weave can be attractively applied to part of a wall when the rest of the wall is a solid base color. A basket weave border near the ceiling in a guest bedroom would complement wicker furniture. Set at chair-rail height, a basket weave border adds interest in a casual dining room or breakfast nook. Soft, muted colors in a monochromatic scheme can add subtle texture to an otherwise dull space.

MATERIALS AND TOOLS

- ❖ Painter's masking tape
- ❖ Drop cloths
- ❖ Paint roller and tray
- ❖ Latex paint for base coat
- ❖ Rubber gloves
- ❖ Water-based glazing liquid
- ❖ Latex paint for glaze mixture
- ❖ Paint bucket and mixing tool
- ❖ Triangular graining tool
- ❖ Clean rags

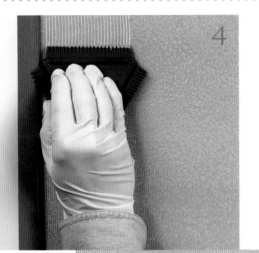

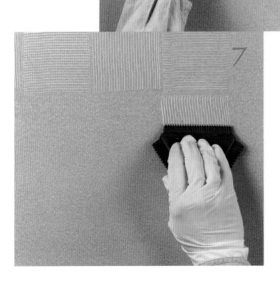

1 Prepare the walls for painting (page 123). Protect the area around the walls with painter's masking tape and drop cloths (page 126). Apply the base coat and let it dry completely.

2 In the bucket, prepare the glaze mixture, mixing one part latex paint with two parts glazing liquid.

3 Apply the glaze in a 2-ft. (0.6 m) wide area from ceiling to floor, using the roller. Make sure the wall surface is evenly covered.

4 Using the fine-toothed side of the triangular graining tool, vertically comb a section from the top corner of the wall downward. The section should only be as deep as the comb is wide, resulting in a square. Lift the tool from the surface.

5 Turn the tool perpendicular to the lines of the first square. Beginning alongside the first square, horizontally comb a square of the same size. Wipe excess glaze from the comb onto clean rags as necessary.

6 Continue combing the top row of squares in the 2-ft. (0.6 m) wide area, alternating vertical and horizontal squares. Leave a 2" (5 cm) wet edge of glaze and move down to the next row, beginning with a horizontal square and continuing to alternate directions. A checkerboard pattern will develop.

7 Apply another strip of glaze alongside the wet edge. Comb a basket-weave column vertically before the wet edge dries. Then continue combing each row horizontally, again leaving a 2" (5 cm) wet edge of glaze.

8 Repeat step 7, moving around the room until all the walls are finished.

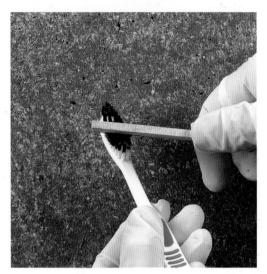

Faux FINISHES

Paint applications that are designed
to mimic other materials are called
faux finishes. In the next seventeen
ways to paint a wall, innovative
methods are used to apply paints,
glazes, and texturizing materials
to create illusions of fabric, stone,
wood, and other natural surfaces.

25 Textured Metallic

RICH METALLIC COLORS applied with dramatic texture produce a finish that has a unique aged appearance. It is best to apply the textured metallic paint finish to a distinct, compact wall area, such as a built-in niche or a slender divider wall between two rooms. A modest alcove wall or the minimal wall space above upper cabinets will come alive when the textured metallic finish is applied.

For the best results, select a brown and green of the same intensity. The "washing" of the light green latex paint over the bronze, copper, and brown creates the hint of metal. Or partner pewter, brushed silver, matte gold, or any other popular metallic hue with a light green latex paint. Because of the textured plaster in this technique, the only way to remove it is to replace the wall board, so practice before you begin.

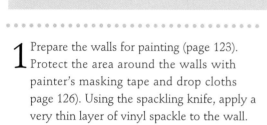

MATERIALS AND TOOLS

- ❖ Painter's masking tape
- ❖ Drop cloths
- ❖ Vinyl spackle
- ❖ Wide plastic spackling knife
- ❖ Rubber gloves
- ❖ Water
- ❖ Sea sponges
- ❖ Brown satin latex paint for base coat
- ❖ Paintbrush
- ❖ Bronze metallic paint
- ❖ Copper metallic paint
- ❖ Light green latex paint
- ❖ Cotton rags

1 Prepare the walls for painting (page 123). Protect the area around the walls with painter's masking tape and drop cloths page 126). Using the spackling knife, apply a very thin layer of vinyl spackle to the wall.

2 Put on rubber gloves. Slightly dampen a sea sponge with water. Beginning at the top of the wall, pull the sponge down over the vinyl spackle to create small ridges. Let the surface dry completely.

3 Apply the brown base coat to the wall, using the paintbrush. Let it dry completely.

4 Dip a clean, damp sea sponge into the bronze metallic paint; dab off excess. Beginning at the top of the wall, apply the bronze paint over the brown base coat, pulling the sponge in vertical strokes. Reload the sponge with paint as needed. Let the surface dry completely.

5 Repeat step 4 using the copper metallic paint. Let the surface dry completely.

6 For a verdigris effect, apply the light green paint as in step 4, but wipe off as much of the excess paint as you desire, using a damp rag.

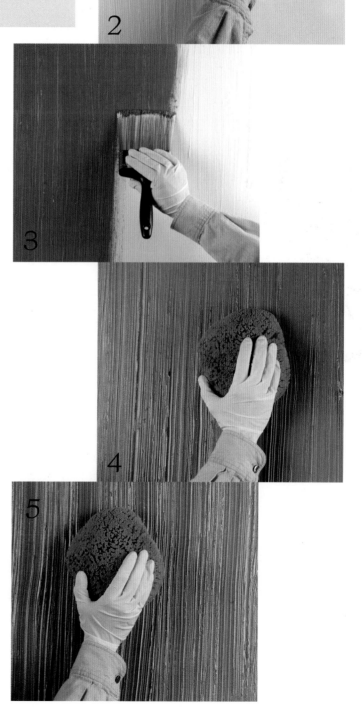

26 Pearl

THE PEARL FINISH casts a soft, white shimmer over the wall surface. The walls appear to subtly change color as you walk by or as the lighting in the room changes.

Pearlescent or opalescent paint is a translucent finishing product, much like a glaze, that is applied over a base coat. It is available in a few white or off-white colors. An additive creates the luster. Because the additive tends to settle to the bottom, the product should be stirred often during application.

Strong colors can be used for the base coat because the sheer pearl finish will soften the color a lot. If a pastel is used for the base coat, the wall will have a soft white shimmer with only a hint of color.

Pearlescent walls can be a stunning focal point around a tub in a master bathroom or as a fireplace wall in a master bedroom. When painted as vertical stripes (page 46), the pearl technique will lend height and drama to a formal living room. The technique is especially striking when used in a contemporary interior that features furnishings with sleek lines and glass or metal surfaces.

MATERIALS AND TOOLS

- ❖ Painter's masking tape
- ❖ Drop cloths
- ❖ Paint roller and tray
- ❖ Semigloss latex paint for base coat
- ❖ Rubber gloves
- ❖ Pearlescent or opalescent paint
- ❖ Paintbrush, 2" (5 cm) wide
- ❖ Block stippler
- ❖ Small edge stippler
- ❖ Clean rags

1 Prepare the walls for painting (page 123). Protect the area around the walls with painter's masking tape and drop cloths (page 126). Apply the base coat and let it dry completely.

2 Put on rubber gloves. Beginning in an upper corner, apply a 2-ft. (0.6 m) square area of pearlescent paint. Use the paintbrush to cut in along the ceiling and wall corner; use the paint roller to fill in the area.

3 Butter the block stippler, as in step 4 on page 41. While the paint is wet, stipple the area with a pouncing action. Move your arm in a circular motion, overlapping the imprints. Leave an unstippled wet edge where the adjacent square will be applied.

4 Repeat steps 2 and 3 in adjacent areas until the entire wall is complete. Wipe excess paint from the stippler onto clean rags, as necessary. Use the edge stippler to stipple the corners and around woodwork.

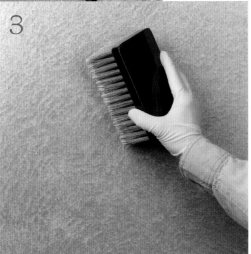

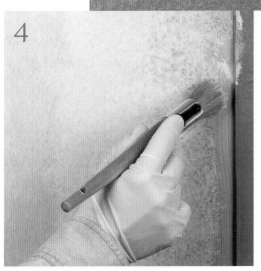

27 Fresco

FRESCO IS AN advanced paint technique that creates a stucco-like textured surface. It is well suited for walls that already have irregularities or imperfections. It is important to work quickly, as the drywall joint compound used to texture the wall dries rapidly. Working with a partner helps to speed transitions from one area of the wall to another.

After drying, the textured surface is painted and color washed (page 14). Light or medium shades of the same color used for the base coat and glaze most dramatically show the fresco's texture. Pale, earth-tone colors are attractive choices for fresco color schemes. Although fresco is found in many rustic and country styled homes, it also provides a warm backdrop for even the most contemporary interior that lacks pattern, color, or texture.

You can change the color of your fresco wall, but the only way to successfully remove the texture is to replace the plasterboard. Therefore, it is essential that you test the application on a small piece of plasterboard to be sure you will like the results.

MATERIALS AND TOOLS

- ❖ Painter's masking tape
- ❖ Drop cloths
- ❖ Rubber gloves
- ❖ Drywall joint compound
- ❖ Wide spackling knife
- ❖ Dust mask
- ❖ Sandpaper
- ❖ Vacuum
- ❖ Drywall primer

- ❖ Paint roller with ¾" (2 cm) nap; tray
- ❖ Latex paint for base coat
- ❖ Paint bucket and mixing tool
- ❖ Water-based glazing liquid
- ❖ Latex paint for glaze mixture
- ❖ Paintbrush, 4" to 6" (10 to 15 cm) wide

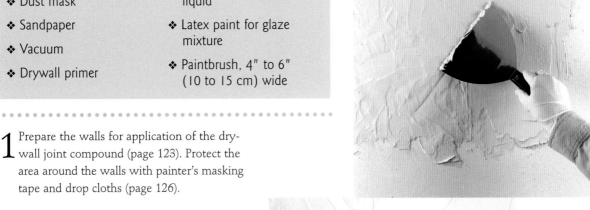

1 Prepare the walls for application of the drywall joint compound (page 123). Protect the area around the walls with painter's masking tape and drop cloths (page 126).

2 Put on rubber gloves. Beginning at the upper corner and working downward, apply an ⅛" (3 mm) layer of compound to the wall with a spackling knife. Use random sweeping motions to produce a rough wall surface. Allow the compound to dry completely.

3 Put on a dust mask and sand down any areas of compound that contain high ridges and bumps, for a smoother look. Vacuum the entire wall.

4 Apply drywall primer to the wall surface, using the roller. Let it dry completely.

5 Apply the base coat to the wall surface, using the roller. Let it dry completely.

6 In the bucket, prepare the glaze mixture, mixing one part latex paint with four parts glazing liquid.

7 Beginning in an upper corner, apply the glaze mixture using the color washing technique on page 14. Allow the base coat to be subtly exposed.

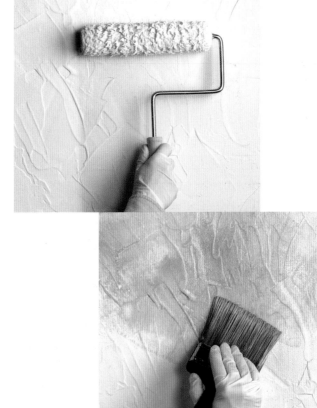

28 Venetian Plaster

VENETIAN PLASTER has the mellow, weathered appearance of old plaster walls that can be found in Italy. This elegant finish is often applied by craftspeople to the walls of upscale retail stores and restaurants because of its architectural interest and durability. Home owners can buy the tinted plasters at paint stores, along with the proper trowels for applying the finish. The three-part process of layering the plaster is easy to learn and forgiving.

Venetian plaster is available in a limited number of colors, usually in earthy, faded, sun-drenched hues.

Trust the color card when choosing a shade of Venetian plaster. Unlike wet paint, which can be a couple of shades lighter than the color represented on the sample card, wet Venetian plaster is about 40 percent darker than the color indicated on the sample card. The true color will develop as the plaster dries.

Venetian plaster is a permanent finish. The wet plaster can be scraped off the wall if you are not satisfied with your results, but after it dries, the only way to successfully remove it is to replace the plasterboard.

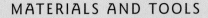

MATERIALS AND TOOLS

- ❖ Painter's masking tape
- ❖ Drop cloths
- ❖ Rubber gloves
- ❖ Primer tinted the same color as the plaster
- ❖ Venetian plaster

- ❖ Small trowel
- ❖ Large trowel
- ❖ Handsanding block with 220-grit and 400-grit sandpapers
- ❖ Clean rags

1 Prepare the walls for the plaster treatment (page 123). Protect the area around the walls with painter's masking tape and drop cloths (page 126). Apply the primer and let it dry completely.

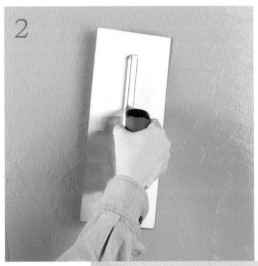

2 Put on rubber gloves. Apply the first thin coat of plaster to a section of the wall using a small trowel. Using the large trowel, smooth out the plaster. Let the plaster dry completely.

3 Apply a second thin coat of plaster, using the small trowel and working in broad criss-cross motions. The walls should appear textured. Allow the second coat of plaster to dry completely.

4 Apply a third and final thin coat of plaster to the wall surface using the large trowel, smoothing it over the second layer. Allow the third coat of plaster to dry completely.

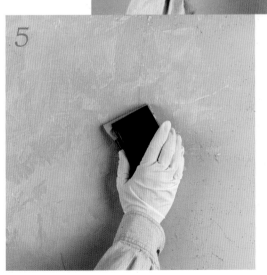

5 Sand the wall very lightly in an up and down motion, using a hand sanding block and 220-grit sandpaper. Then sand with 400-grit sandpaper to subtly polish the top coat of the plaster.

6 Wipe off the plaster dust, using a slightly damp rag.

29 Denim

PAINT GLAZE MANIPULATED with a special brush can produce the distinct appearance of worn denim fabric. Fine vertical and horizontal lines created in the glaze mimic the weave of this casual cotton fabric.

The denim technique is a favorite for the family room, game room, and other relaxed family spaces. It is often used in children's and teens' bedrooms and bathrooms. The denim finish can be attractively customized by hand painting "stitches," "seams," or "pockets" as they appear on denim clothing. Team the denim wall finish with plaids and floral upholstered furnishings and fabrics.

Although it is most recognizable when it appears in classic blue shades, the denim technique can be applied in a variety of colors. Consider pastel colors such as soft pinks, pale yellows, or gentle peaches.

1 Prepare the walls for painting (page 123). Protect the area around the walls with painter's masking tape and drop cloths (page 126). Apply the base coat and let it dry completely.

2 Put on rubber gloves. In a bucket, prepare the first glaze, mixing two parts of the first paint color with two parts glazing liquid and one part water.

3 Beginning at the top of the wall, apply the glaze horizontally in an 18" (46 cm) wide strip, using the roller.

4 While the glaze is wet, drag the denim weaver brush or wallpaper brush horizontally through the glaze in continuous strokes from corner to corner. Wipe excess glaze from the brush onto rags after each stroke.

5 Repeat steps 3 and 4, working from top to bottom on each wall. Much of the neutral base coat should show through the glaze. Allow the glaze to dry completely.

6 In another bucket, prepare the second glaze, mixing equal amounts of the darker color, glazing liquid, and water. Note that the increase in the amount of water will produce a thinner mixture.

7 Beginning in the top corner, apply the glaze and drag through it as in steps 3 and 4, but working vertically. Some of the background color and much of the first glaze color should show through.

30 Linen

DRAGGING A BRUSH through wet glaze in horizontal and vertical strokes creates the woven look of linen. This finish is soft and subtle and will not compete with heavily patterned fabrics, ornate furnishings, or artwork and collections found in the room.

The most effective colors for this technique resemble actual linen fabric. Consider using light, natural tones, such as soft sand and wheat, or pale pastels, such as muted yellows and washed blues.

The linen paint finish is versatile enough to be used throughout the home and teamed with several styles of décor. Though commonly used in cottage style or country settings, the linen finish also works in contemporary spaces. This technique can be an attractive partner to wide vertical stripes (page 46) in adjacent rooms with similar color schemes.

In preparation for applying the linen paint finish, the walls are taped off in vertical sections that mimic the width of actual linen fabric. Thin lines of deeper color where the sections overlap will appear as seams in the fabric, adding to the illusion that the walls are covered with linen.

1 Prepare the walls for painting (page 123). Protect the area around the walls with painter's masking tape and drop cloths (page 126). Apply the base coat and let it dry completely.

2 Divide the room into a series of vertical sections that you can work with easily and quickly from top to bottom. Using painter's tape, mask off every other section.

3 Put on rubber gloves. In the bucket, prepare the glaze, mixing five parts glazing liquid with one part paint. Apply the glaze mixture onto the first wall section using the roller. While the glaze is still wet, drag the linen weaver brush in long horizontal strokes, back and forth, through the entire section. Wipe off excess glaze from the brush with a lint-free cloth after each stroke.

4 Turn the brush and drag it through the glaze in long vertical strokes, from top to bottom.

5 Repeat steps 3 and 4 for each alternating wall section. Remove the tape and allow each section to dry completely.

6 Mask off the painted sections, positioning the tape 1/8" (3 mm) inside the painted edges. As the glaze overlaps in these thin lines, it will create the look of seams. Repeat steps 3 and 4 in the remaining sections. Remove the tape and let the glaze dry completely.

31 Parchment

RICH COLORS and sophisticated dimensional texture are combined in a parchment finish. Crumpled tissue paper is sealed into the paint, leaving a network of wrinkled ridges. The wall becomes a delight to the eye and invites admiring touches. Since the paper is sealed into the paint, the wall can be touched often, and even wiped with a damp cloth when necessary, without fear of damaging the finish.

Parchment, a popular wall treatment in many designer showcase homes, can

be incorporated tastefully into any style of décor. Deep, strong colors highlight the dimension of the wrinkled ridges. Consider burgundy, dark brown, maroon, plum, black, or forest green. Light, natural tans and creams will create a subdued appearance. A slightly darker color-wash finish can be added to emphasize the texture.

Decide carefully where to use the parchment finish, as removing it from walls requires replacing the plasterboard.

MATERIALS AND TOOLS

- Painter's masking tape
- Drop cloths
- Tissue paper, enough to cover the wall in a single layer
- Paint roller and tray
- Latex paint for base coat
- Rubber gloves
- Paint bucket and mixing tool, optional
- Satin latex paint for color washing glaze, optional
- Water-based glazing liquid, optional
- Paintbrush, 4" to 6" (10 to 15 cm) wide, optional

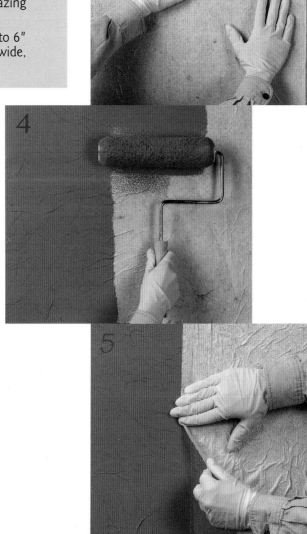

1 Prepare the walls for painting (page 123). Protect the area around the walls with painter's masking tape and drop cloths (page 126).

2 Scrunch up whole pieces of tissue paper and set them aside.

3 Put on rubber gloves. Beginning in an upper corner, apply the base-coat paint to an area slightly larger than a sheet of tissue paper, using the roller. While the paint is wet, open up a sheet of crumpled tissue paper and apply it to the wall, using your hands to smooth the paper into the wet paint. Leave small crinkles in a random pattern.

4 Roll over the surface carefully with a second coat of the base-coat paint.

5 Repeat steps 3 and 4, slightly overlapping the tissue papers until the entire surface has been covered evenly and completely. Let the wall dry completely.

6 If an aged look is desired, apply a colorwash finish, following steps 2 to 5 on page 15.

32 Grass Cloth

WOVEN GRASS WALL COVERINGS are an expensive investment, but you can create the same look with paint and a squeegee. The grass cloth paint technique is a variation of combing (page 28). Sawtooth points cut into the edge of a rubber squeegee manipulate the top coat of paint, removing fine lines of color to expose the base coat. The walls are taped off in sections similar in width to wallpaper. When the painting is complete, narrow lines of color where the sections overlap resemble butted wallpaper seams.

For a realistic appearance, select paint colors, such as sand and wheat, that closely resemble natural grasses. Because of the earthy nature of the technique, grass cloth walls work well in a casual sunroom where plants and natural textures are key design elements. The grass cloth look when married to rich reds and classic black exudes luxurious elegance in an Asian or other ethnically inspired décor.

The walls will have to be sanded and primed before repainting at a later date.

MATERIALS AND TOOLS

- ❖ Painter's masking tape
- ❖ Drop cloths
- ❖ Paint roller and tray
- ❖ Latex paint for base coat
- ❖ Pencil
- ❖ Long carpenter's level
- ❖ Scissors
- ❖ Window squeegee
- ❖ Rubber gloves
- ❖ Latex paint for top coat
- ❖ Sash brush
- ❖ Small paint comb
- ❖ Clean rags

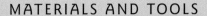

1 Prepare the walls for painting (page 123). Protect the area around the walls with painter's masking tape and drop cloths (page 126). Apply the base coat and let it dry completely.

2 Using the pencil, mark off 3-ft. (1 m) vertical panels around the room. Pencil in the edge lines with the level. Tape off every other panel.

3 Using the scissors, cut the squeegee into a sawtooth pattern, with pointed teeth about 1/4" (6 mm) apart.

4 Put on rubber gloves. Cut in the top and bottom of the panel with the top-coat paint, using the sash brush. Immediately fill in the rest of the panel, using the paint roller.

5 Draw the squeegee across the painted panel horizontally, beginning at the top and moving downward. Overlap the passes to create a grass cloth look. After each pass, wipe excess paint from the squeegee onto clean rags. Use a small paint comb for hard-to-reach areas like corners, and around switches and outlets. Remove the tape before the paint dries.

6 Repeat steps 4 and 5 for each alternating wall section. Allow each section to dry completely.

7 Mask off the painted sections, positioning the tape 1/8" (3 mm) inside the painted edges. As the paint overlaps in these thin lines, it will create the look of seams in wallpaper. Repeat steps 4 and 5 in the remaining sections. Remove the tape and let the paint dry completely.

33 Bamboo

THIS TECHNIQUE REPLICATES the look of slender, graceful bamboo stalks. A special paint tool, called a Color Shaper, is drawn through the wet top coat to remove slim lines of paint. The realistic look is enhanced by leaving short breaks in the lines, like the divisions in real bamboo, and by creatively overlapping and angling some of the stalks.

This look works well with Asian and tropical themes. It also works well with contemporary interiors.

For an authentic appearance, use a base-coat color in a natural, woody tone that closely resembles actual bamboo. A realistic effect will be created if the top-coat color is a slightly darker shade than the base coat. An entire room of bamboo stalks would be overwhelming, so limit the effect to a focal corner or wall, or leave wide, irregularly spaced gaps of plain painted wall between clusters of stalks.

MATERIALS AND TOOLS

- ❖ Painter's masking tape
- ❖ Drop cloths
- ❖ Paint roller and tray
- ❖ Satin latex paint for base coat
- ❖ Rubber gloves
- ❖ Latex paint for top coat
- ❖ Flat Color Shaper, 1" (2.5 cm) wide
- ❖ Clean rags

1 Prepare the walls for painting (page 123). Protect the area around the walls with painter's masking tape and drop cloths (page 126). Apply the base coat and let it dry completely.

2 Put on rubber gloves. Using the top-coat paint, roll approximately two widths of the roller onto the wall, creating a vertical strip. Beginning at the top of the wall, pull the Color Shaper downward through the wet paint in a straight, slightly angled line, removing some of the paint. Break the line every 12" to 18" (30.5 to 46 cm), leave a short space, and begin again, to mimic the divisions in a real bamboo stalk. After completing the stalk, wipe excess paint from the tool onto clean rags.

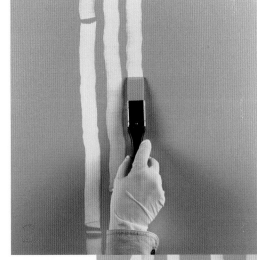

3 Repeat step 2 several times in the same strip of wet paint, pulling the tool at slightly different angles and crisscrossing some of the stalks.

4 Paint a small section of the top-coat color and leave it plain. Then repeat steps 2 and 3 alongside the plain section. Continue until all of the walls are complete.

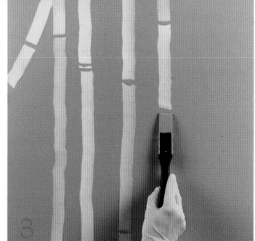

34 Suede

THE SUEDE PAINT FINISH provides the soft, grainy visual texture of real suede and brings a cozy feeling to a room. Suede-finish latex paint contains a special additive that produces the characteristic grainy appearance. Suede-finish latex paint base is available from several paint manufacturers and can be tinted to any color. Because the additive tends to settle to the bottom, the product should be stirred often during application.

For a traditional suede appearance, select from any of the classic earthy colors that resemble real suede: shades of brown, cream, sand, and tan, or variations of red such as cinnamon, clay, or terra cotta.

The suede finish is a technique that easily adapts to many styles of décor, ranging from traditional to rustic to contemporary to Southwestern. Topped with an elegant wallpaper border, the suede finish offers high style in a formal dining area. Dark and dramatic suede colors add distinction to a home library. The appearance of suede walls lends instant texture to a compact space.

- ❖ Painter's masking tape
- ❖ Drop cloths
- ❖ Primer, tinted to the top-coat color
- ❖ Paint roller with spatter guard and tray

- ❖ Suede-finish latex paint
- ❖ Small paintbrush for cutting in
- ❖ Foam roller
- ❖ Paintbrush, 4" (10 cm) wide

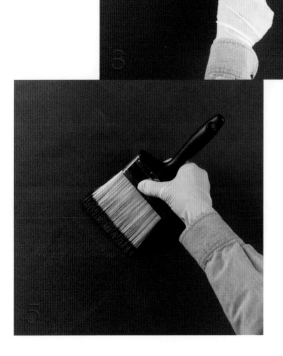

1 Prepare the walls for painting (page 123). Protect the area around the walls with painter's masking tape and drop cloths (page 126). Apply the tinted primer as the base coat. Let the primer dry completely.

2 Load the small paintbrush with the suede paint and cut in around the ceiling and wall edges in a 2-ft (.06 m) square area. Load the foam roller and fill in the square, rolling in a zigzag pattern.

3 Continue down to the next 2-ft (.06 m) square section and repeat the process until the vertical strip of wall is filled in with paint. Smooth and even the painted section by slowly rolling the foam roller over the section in long vertical strokes.

4 Repeat steps 2 and 3 until the entire wall is painted with the first coat. Allow to dry completely.

5 Using the 4" (10 cm) paintbrush, apply a second coat of suede paint, in crosshatch strokes over the entire wall. Begin in the upper corner and work from top to bottom, then left to right. This will produce the soft shading characteristic of suede.

35 Leather

IN THIS LEATHER painting technique, plastic sheeting, in the form of garbage bags, is used to manipulate the glaze and leave an imprint in the paint that imitates the fine cracks and wrinkled texture apparent in aged leather. To obtain a true leather appearance, choose deep, rich colors. Deep slate grays and rich chocolate browns offer realistic interpretations of actual leather. The most effective results are produced with two distinctly different shades of the same color, using the lighter shade for the base coat and the darker shade for the glaze.

Walls painted with the leather technique are traditional favorites for studies or home offices. However, do not overlook the possibility of using the leather finish in an unexpected area of the home, such as a bathroom or foyer. It's also hip in a teenager's bedroom!

MATERIALS AND TOOLS

- ❖ Painter's masking tape
- ❖ Drop cloths
- ❖ Paint roller and tray
- ❖ Latex paint for base coat
- ❖ Scissors
- ❖ Large plastic garbage bags
- ❖ Rubber gloves
- ❖ Paint bucket and mixing tool
- ❖ Latex paint for top coat
- ❖ Water-based glazing liquid
- ❖ Paintbrush

1 Prepare the walls for painting (page 123). Protect the area around the walls with painter's masking tape and drop cloths (page 126). Apply the base coat and let it dry completely.

2 Cut plastic garbage bags apart at the sides and bottom. You will need enough pieces to cover the entire wall. Stack the pieces where you can easily reach them as you work.

3 Put on rubber gloves. In a bucket, prepare the glaze, mixing one part paint with one part glazing liquid.

4 Beginning at an upper corner, apply glaze to the wall in an area slightly larger than one piece of plastic. Use the brush for cutting in and the paint roller for filling in the area.

5 Smooth a sheet of plastic directly into the wet glaze. Scrunch it slightly so there are a few wrinkles in the plastic.

6 Peel the plastic from the wall. The plastic will lift some of the glaze from the wall and leave a slightly wrinkled appearance. Dispose of the plastic.

7 Repeat steps 4 to 6 in adjacent areas until the entire wall is complete.

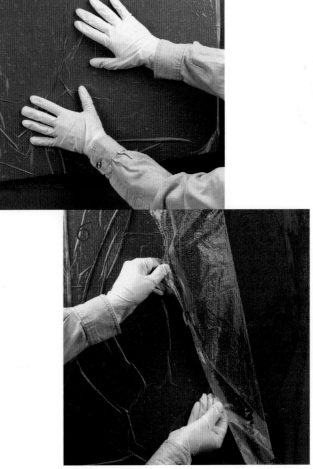

36 Wood Graining

HANDSOME, REALISTIC wood-grain finishes can be painted with a specialty tool called a wood-graining rocker. Curved grooves in the rubber surface of the rocker create the characteristic whorls and lines as the tool is drawn through wet paint. Part of the charm of the technique is slight imperfections, which further enhance the authenticity.

Available craft stores and home improvement centers, the wood-graining tool requires a steady hand. It is important to practice on a sample board before graining the wall to get a feel for the tool. Because you must work quickly on the wet surface, it is essential to limit the technique to small wall spaces, such as under the chair rail in a home library, home office, or dining room.

To achieve a realistic effect, use honey, tan, and other shades of brown found in golden oaks, light maples, dark cherry, and other real woods. Match the base-coat color to the underlying hue of the wood, and use a darker tone for the top coat. Unexpected bright hues or soft pastels to create an offbeat, unconventional look.

1 Prepare the walls for painting (page 123). Protect the area around the walls with painter's masking tape and drop cloths (page 126). Apply the base coat and let it dry completely.

2 Put on rubber gloves. Roll the top-coat paint onto the wall in a narrow strip (about the width of the roller) from top to bottom. Starting at the top, immediately slide the wood-graining tool downward through the paint, rocking it slowly back and forth in one continuous motion, to create oval markings. Wipe the excess paint from the tool onto clean rags after each full stroke.

3 Wood-grain the rest of the painted strip, working in continuous strokes that overlap slightly, varying the rocking rhythm to stagger the markings.

4 Repeat steps 2 and 3 in adjacent narrow strips until the entire area is complete.

37 Granite

THE GRANITE TECHNIQUE combines a three-color sponging process with spattering to produce a multicolored, speckled surface that mimics natural granite stone.

The most effective color choices for this technique are those found in real granite. Traditional granite color combinations include black with gray flecks, dark green with gold flecks, and tan with dark brown and cinnamon flecks. It is recommended that you begin sponging with the darkest color first, as it is easier to adjust the depth of color by subsequently adding the lighter colors.

Natural granite is an increasingly popular surface in bathroom and kitchen spaces. The granite paint technique can be used to handsomely coordinate with natural granite back-splashes and countertops. The granite paint technique may be applied to a variety of styles of décor in spaces ranging from the master bathroom to the sunroom, craft room, or laundry room.

MATERIALS AND TOOLS

- ❖ Painter's masking tape
- ❖ Drop cloths
- ❖ Paint roller and tray
- ❖ Satin latex paint for base coat
- ❖ Rubber gloves

- ❖ Satin water-based glazing liquid
- ❖ Latex paint in three colors (dark, medium, and light) and black for glazes
- ❖ Jars with lids for mixing glazes
- ❖ Disposable aluminum pans

- ❖ Large sea sponges
- ❖ Bucket of water
- ❖ Stiff-bristle brush, such as a toothbrush
- ❖ Spatter stick
- ❖ Semigloss varnish

1 Prepare the walls for painting (page 123). Protect the area around the walls with painter's masking tape and drop cloths (page 126). Apply the base coat and let it dry completely.

2 Put on rubber gloves. Mix the three colored glazes in separate jars, following the manufacturer's directions. Pour small amounts of each glaze into disposable pans. Dip a damp sea sponge into the darkest glaze. Sponge the glaze onto the wall lightly and evenly, working in a 3-ft. (1 m) square area. Allow much of the base coat to show through.

3 Dip the sponge into the medium glaze. Sponge the glaze onto the same area lightly and evenly, allowing some of the base coat and much of the first glaze to show through.

4 Dip the sponge into the light glaze. Sponge the glaze onto the same area lightly and evenly, allowing small peeks of the base coat and much of the first two glazes to show through. The colors will begin to blend together slightly.

5 Stand back from the wall and decide where you would like to add darker or lighter areas of color. Sponge on more color as desired, adding the dark glaze first, then the medium glaze, and finally the light glaze. Let the glaze dry completely.

6 Repeat steps 2 to 5 in adjacent areas until the entire wall is finished.

7 Mix the black glaze. Spatter (page 42) it on sparingly, using the stiff-bristle brush. Spatter any of the other color glazes, creating areas of greater and lesser density of color. Let the glaze dry completely.

8 Apply several coats of varnish, allowing the wall to dry completely between coats.

38 Stone Blocks

THIS APPLICATION CREATES the look of stone blocks separated by grout lines. Painted stone blocks can add interesting visual texture to a variety of interiors. Consider applying the technique to a front entry or surrounding a cozy breakfast nook. Irregular blocks produce a more authentic, rustic look for country styled spaces. Additional detail can be achieved by hand painting cracks and fissure lines in the individual stone blocks.

Subtle colors that mimic the palette of natural stone are the best choices for this technique. Choose warm neutrals and natural stone colors such as sand, cream, and tan, as well as various shades of brown, gray, and putty.

The grout lines are created by first applying a grid of narrow masking tape to the wall and then painting over the entire surface. The lines are revealed when the tape is removed. Though the texture is mostly visual, there will be low ridges in the surface along the grout lines. Therefore, the wall will have to be sanded and primed before it can be repainted later.

MATERIALS AND TOOLS

- ❖ Painter's masking tape
- ❖ Drop cloths
- ❖ Paint roller and tray
- ❖ Cream flat latex paint for base coat
- ❖ Tape measure
- ❖ Pencil

- ❖ Carpenter's or laser level
- ❖ Painter's masking tape, ¼" (6 mm) wide
- ❖ Craft knife
- ❖ Rubber gloves
- ❖ Flat water-based glazing liquid

- ❖ Flat latex paint in three earth-tone colors
- ❖ Jars with lids for mixing glazes
- ❖ Foam applicator or paintbrush
- ❖ Newspaper

1 Prepare walls for painting (page 123). Protect the area around the walls with painter's masking tape and drop cloths (page 126). Apply the base coat and let it dry completely.

2 Mark a pattern of blocks with the tape measure, pencil, and carpenter's level or laser level. Apply narrow masking tape over the pencil lines, cutting ends and corners neatly with the craft knife.

3 Put on rubber gloves. Mix the three earth-tone glazes in separate jars, following the manufacturer's directions. Apply the earth-tone glazes in random strokes over a 3-ft. (1 m) square area, using the foam applicator or paintbrush. Allow some of the base coat to show through.

4 Fold a sheet of newspaper to several layers. Press it flat against the wall into the glaze. Lift the paper, removing some of the glaze. Continue to press and lift the newspaper throughout the area, turning the paper in different directions to blend the colors roughly. If the paper gets saturated, refold it so a fresh layer is exposed.

5 Add more color to an area by spreading glaze on the newspaper and pressing it against the wall. Repeat as necessary until the desired effect is achieved. Leave some dark accent areas and some light spots.

6 Repeat steps 3 to 5 in adjacent areas until the entire wall is finished.

7 Carefully and slowly remove the tape, beginning at one end of the wall. The base-

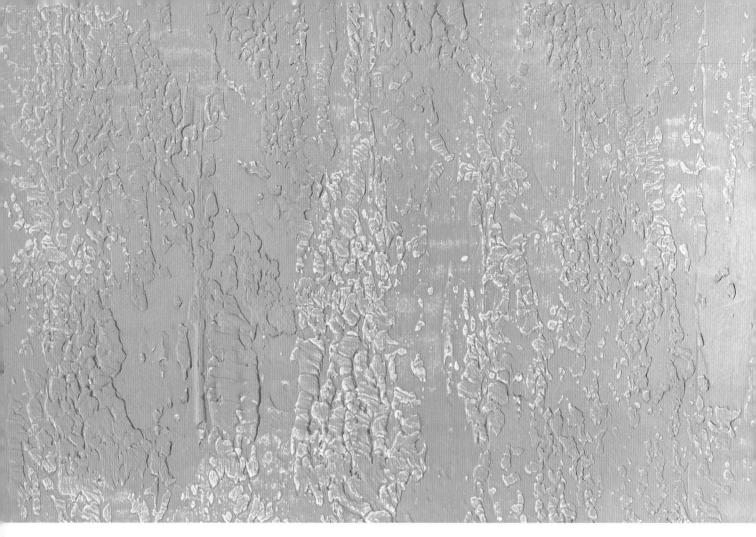

39 Fossil Rock

THE FOSSIL ROCK finish is similar to a classic technique known as "knock down." It is a popular finish for ceilings but is increasingly used on interior walls as well. Drywall joint compound is roughly applied to the wall with a stippler. Then the rugged texture is flattened slightly by drawing a painter's spatula over the compound, leaving a surface that resembles weathered limestone.

Working with drywall compound has distinct advantages. The compound masks flaws and imperfections in the existing wall. It is a flexible medium that remains wet for approximately an hour, so you can remove or rework a section that doesn't look right. Once the compound dries, however, the only way to successfully remove it is to replace the plasterboard.

Color depth can be achieved with various decorative paint techniques, including color washing (page 14), overlaying of color (page 16), or double-roller painting (page 22).

While perfect in a home that proudly displays vintage collectibles and antiques or in a rustic styled space, the fossil rock technique also provides the illusion of instant age for a new home that needs a few timeworn touches.

1 Prepare the walls for application of the drywall joint compound (page 123). Protect the area around the walls with painter's masking tape and drop cloths (page 126).

2 Put on rubber gloves. Dip the stippler into the bucket of joint compound and load it with a generous amount. Apply the compound to the wall surface as evenly as possible using the stippler.

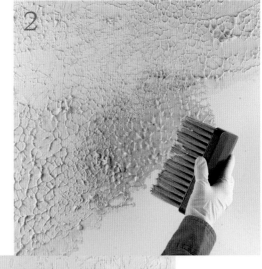

3 Beginning at the top of the wall and working downward, gently drag the spatula over the compound, smoothing down the peaks of the stipples on the wall.

4 Clean the excess compound off the spatula by scraping it on the edge of the mud tray after each pass.

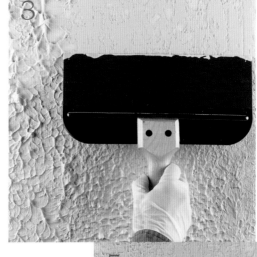

5 Overlap each section slightly and work in 2-ft. (0.6 m) sections downward on the wall. Continue until the wall surface is complete, and let the compound dry completely.

6 Prime the wall surface, and let the primer dry completely.

7 Apply the paint or glaze to the wall surface, using one of the techniques mentioned opposite, and let it dry completely.

40 Clouds

WHAT BETTER WAY to create a calming space for rest or relaxation than by applying gentle painted clouds to the wall? Although often used to portray an airplane or space theme in a nursery or child's bedroom, bathroom, or playroom, clouds can add instant whimsy to other spaces, such as a combination guest room/home office or front entrance.

You can use them near the top of a wall and extend to the ceiling. Sky blue or soft aqua for the base coat and various shades of white and pale grays for the clouds will create a natural appearance. Vary the size and shape of the clouds, overlapping some and spacing them randomly for best effect. To add more depth to the sponged clouds, the background wall color can also be color washed (page 14) or double rolled (page 22).

For a unique twist in a cloud-inspired room, liven up the soothing space by introducing contrasting bold red accents in upholstered furnishings and fabrics. The powerful punch of red (when used in small doses) lends a zesty spirit to the area.

3

- ❖ Painter's masking tape
- ❖ Drop cloths
- ❖ Paint roller and tray
- ❖ Blue satin latex paint for base coat
- ❖ Rubber gloves
- ❖ Two containers for mixing glazes

- ❖ White and gray satin latex paint for clouds
- ❖ Water-based glazing liquid
- ❖ Foam applicators, 2″ and 4″ (5 cm and 10 cm) wide
- ❖ Natural sea sponge
- ❖ Bucket of water

1 Prepare the walls for painting (page 123). Protect the area around the walls with painter's masking tape and drop cloths (page 126). Apply the base coat and let it dry completely.

2 Put on rubber gloves. Prepare the glazes, mixing equal amounts of glazing liquid and white paint in one container, and equal amounts of glazing liquid and gray paint in the other container.

3 Apply an arch of white glaze mixture to the wall, using the wide foam applicator. Apply a shorter arch of gray glaze mixture under the white one, using the narrow applicator.

4 Soak the sponge in water and squeeze tightly so the sponge is damp. Pat the sponge over the arches, softening the glaze into a cloud-like, translucent form. Blend the gray into the white to create natural-looking shadows.

5 Repeat steps 3 and 4 for each cloud, varying the sizes and shapes and scattering them randomly over the upper third of the walls. Rinse out the sponge as it becomes clogged with paint.

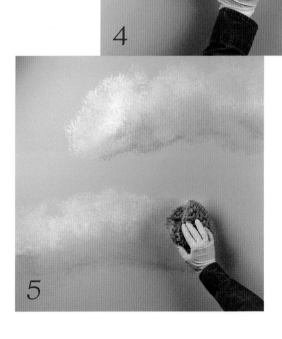

5

41 Crackle

TIMEWORN, WEATHERED WALLS result from the crackle technique, which produces hairline cracks in a random pattern. Timing is very important with crackling, so be sure to read the manufacturer's directions carefully and test the technique before you begin. Crackling is most effective and easiest to accomplish on small, isolated wall areas. To remove or paint over a crackled finish, the wall has to be sanded smooth first.

Crackling can produce striking color combinations. To enhance the success of the finish, it is important to select a base-coat color that will show through the cracks and contrast with the top coat. The more dramatic the color contrast, the more dynamic the crackle effect will appear on the wall.

A wonderful complement to a Western style ranch or rustic log home, the technique also comfortably fits into a historic home with vintage collections and antiques. Particularly suitable for a farmhouse kitchen, the technique can also be applied to coordinating furnishings.

MATERIALS AND TOOLS

- ❖ Painter's masking tape
- ❖ Drop cloths
- ❖ Paint roller and tray
- ❖ Paintbrush
- ❖ Satin latex paint for base coat
- ❖ Rubber gloves

- ❖ Crackle medium
- ❖ Wide paintbrush
- ❖ Latex paint for top coat
- ❖ Sealant recommended by manufacturer of crackle medium

1 Prepare the walls for painting (page 123). Protect the area around the walls with painter's masking tape and drop cloths (page 126). Apply the base coat and let it dry completely.

2 Using the crackle medium, cut in the edges of the wall with the paintbrush. Roll the crackle medium onto the remainder of the wall with the paint roller. Allow the wall to dry for the amount of time recommended by the crackle medium manufacturer (usually about 30 minutes).

3 Apply the top coat of paint over the crackle medium, using the wide paintbrush. Work quickly, beginning at the ceiling and moving downward toward the floor. Apply the paint in segments. Be careful not to overlap the sections, which can result in removing the crackle finish from the wall surface.

4 Allow to dry completely. Seal the crackle finish with a sealant recommended by the crackle medium manufacturer.

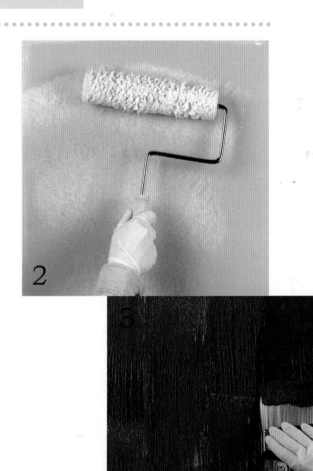

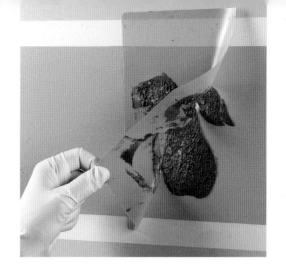

Wall EMBELLISHMENTS

Some walls are places for hanging art; other walls *are* the artwork. The next nine ways to paint a wall include the application of images and designs using a variety of methods, mediums, and tools. With a little creativity and some paint, you can make a masterpiece.

42 | Stamping

STAMPING PROVIDES an attractive accent in a wide range of decorating styles. Rubber stamps suitable for stamping walls are available in craft stores and decorating centers. Fruit and vegetable motifs can be stamped onto a prominent kitchen wall. Modern geometric designs can be stamped onto a wall that adjoins a staircase in a contemporary home. Stamping over a sponged, color-washed, or other background finish produces a subtle elegance in a formal dining room or master bedroom.

Stamping is fun and easy for even a beginning painter, and cleanup is a breeze. It is most effective on smooth wall surfaces. Designs can be applied in classic striped patterns both horizontally and vertically. Motifs can also be stamped in polka-dot fashion on the wall. Used on the walls of an offbeat art studio or child's playroom, random stamping can be a memorable family project. An oversized, bold stamp, such as a musical note or an electric guitar, used with a vivid color produces an energetic effect when used in a music-loving teenager's bedroom.

MATERIALS AND TOOLS

- ❖ Painter's masking tape
- ❖ Drop cloths
- ❖ Paint roller and tray
- ❖ Latex paint for base coat
- ❖ Rubber gloves
- ❖ Paper plate
- ❖ Small foam roller
- ❖ Foam-mounted stamps in desired motifs
- ❖ Acrylic paint in desired colors for stamping
- ❖ Artist's paintbrush

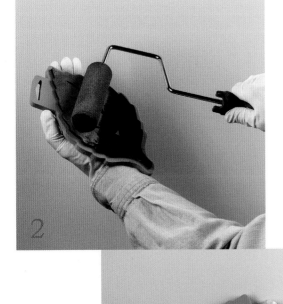

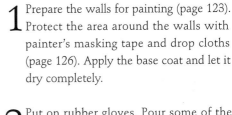

1 Prepare the walls for painting (page 123). Protect the area around the walls with painter's masking tape and drop cloths (page 126). Apply the base coat and let it dry completely.

2 Put on rubber gloves. Pour some of the acrylic paint onto a paper plate. Using the small foam roller, apply an even layer of paint onto the raised surface of the stamp.

3 Press a stamp onto the wall, applying even pressure to the back of the stamp. Carefully lift the stamp from the wall.

4 Repeat steps 2 and 3 for each stamped image.

5 Use the artist's paintbrush to touch up any areas that did not stamp completely as soon as you have finished stamping.

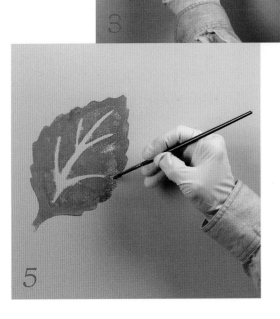

43 Reverse Stamping

IN THE PROCESS of reverse stamping, a sponge shape is pressed into wet glaze, absorbing and lifting the glaze so the base coat shows through. A fun activity and suitable weekend project, reverse stamping may involve all members of the family.

Consider the existing color scheme in the space before selecting the colors for this technique. The most effective reverse-stamping color schemes use the darker hue for the base-coat color and a lighter color for the glaze.

Reverse stamping can easily be incorporated into any style of décor and in any area of a home. Stamps in any shape can be cut from compressed cellulose sponges, available at craft stores. Whimsical juvenile stamps can decorate the walls of a child's bedroom or bathroom. Stamps of fruits, vegetables, and other foods could enhance the walls of a walk-in kitchen pantry. The possibilities are endless.

1 Prepare the walls for painting (page 123). Protect the area around the walls with painter's masking tape and drop cloths (page 126). Apply the base coat and let it dry completely.

2 Draw the desired designs onto the compressed sponges and cut them out. Dip them in water to make them expand. Wring them out.

3 Put on rubber gloves. In the bucket, prepare the glaze, mixing one part latex paint with one part glazing liquid.

4 Beginning in an upper corner, apply glaze to the wall in a 4-ft. (1.2 m) square area, using the paintbrush to cut in and the roller to fill in the area.

5 Press a sponge shape into the glaze and immediately lift it off. The sponge will pick up some of the glaze, leaving a slightly blurry negative image as the base coat comes through.

6 Repeat the reverse stamping with the sponge, flipping to the clean side when necessary, until it is too saturated with glaze to pick up more. Rinse the sponge in the bucket of water.

7 Repeat steps 4 to 6 until the wall is complete.

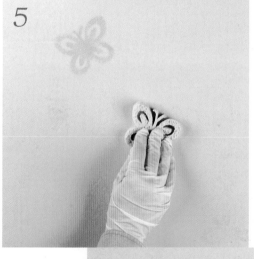

44 Stenciling

STENCILS ADD a personal touch to a room. Decorator stencils are available in nearly every imaginable motif and can enhance many décors throughout the home.

Today's hottest stencils have popular design motifs like Mediterranean, Aztec, and English gardens. Stencils are often applied over decorative paint finishes, such as color washing. A stenciled design can define an architectural feature—highlighting a fireplace mantel—or can be repeated to make a border.

Quality supplies and proper care of stencils are key. Low-tack repositionable spray adhesive, quality stiff-bristle stencil brushes, and quick-drying and easy-to-clean acrylic paints are critical. Any mistakes made when stenciling can be quickly wiped away with a damp cloth. Then, simply allow the area to dry and restencil. Clean brushes with warm water right after use and allow them to air-dry. Store brushes in a container with their bristles up. Clean stencils right after use and dry them carefully with a towel. Store stencils flat to prevent bending.

- ❖ Painter's masking tape
- ❖ Drop cloths
- ❖ Latex paint for base coat
- ❖ Stencils in desired motifs
- ❖ Pencil

- ❖ Yardstick and level
- ❖ Stencil adhesive spray
- ❖ Acrylic paint in desired colors
- ❖ Paper plates, one for each color

- ❖ Stenciling brushes, one for each color
- ❖ Cotton cloth
- ❖ Water

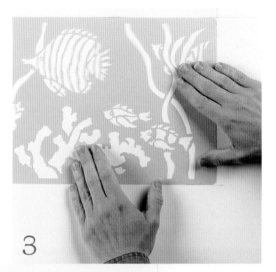

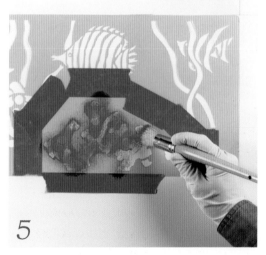

1 Prepare the walls for painting (page 123). Protect the area around the walls with painter's masking tape and drop cloths (page 126). Apply the base coat and let it dry completely.

2 If you are stenciling in a repeated motif, determine where you will begin to stencil. Use pencil marks to mark where the stencils will be placed.

3 Lightly spray adhesive on the back of the stencil and let it set for a few minutes, until it becomes tacky. Line up the center of the stencil with the center of the wall surface and press it against the wall in the desired position.

4 Mask off any design areas you don't want to stencil. Pour the first color of acrylic paint onto a paper plate. Gently dip the brush into the paint and dab off any excess.

5 Using a dabbing motion, lightly swirl the paint over the stencil's open portions. Work from one edge of the stencil toward the opposite edge. Reload the brush as necessary and complete the first stencil motif. To create shading, apply paint more heavily around the outer edges of each opening, leaving highlights in the centers.

6 Carefully remove the stencil and touch up any paint seepage. Allow the motif just painted to dry completely.

7 Reposition the stencil in the next location on the wall, using the pencil marks as a guide. Repeat steps 5 and 6 until you have achieved the desired look for your walls. Clean the stencil and reapply the adhesive as necessary.

45 Dimensional Stenciling

DIMENSIONAL STENCILING creates a raised design through a plastic stencil and an embossing medium. The key is to apply the embossing material evenly over the stencil, building depth in thin layers. Stencils with large motifs and no fine details work best. Various embossing mediums can be used, including dimensional craft paint, as used above, and Venetian plaster (page 72). Both mediums are precolored, though dimensional craft paint can be purchased in much smaller quantities. Unpigmented mediums, such as artist's gels and modeling pastes, can also be used. Follow the manufacturer's directions for adding color.

Dimensional stenciling can be used in place of moldings near the ceiling or floor, under a chair rail, or above a backsplash. The flexibility of the stencil allows you to apply a design around a curve. Monochromatic looks with dimensional stencils that are similar in color to the base coat lend quiet elegance. Using an embossing medium that contrasts with the base coat accentuates the stenciled motif.

MATERIALS AND TOOLS

- ❖ Painter's masking tape
- ❖ Drop cloths
- ❖ Paint roller and tray
- ❖ Latex paint for base coat
- ❖ Pencil
- ❖ Stencil spray adhesive
- ❖ Small trowels
- ❖ Embossing medium
- ❖ Single overlay heavy-duty stencil motif

1 Prepare the walls for painting (page 123). Protect the area around the walls with painter's masking tape and drop cloths (page 126). Apply the base coat and let it dry completely. Lightly mark with a pencil where your stenciled designs will appear on the wall.

2 Holding the can of stencil spray adhesive at least 12" (30.5 cm) away, lightly mist the back of the stencil to ensure a tight seal around the edges of the design. Allow the adhesive to set up for a minute. Affix the stencil to the wall.

3 Apply a small amount of embossing medium to the trowel. Holding the trowel parallel to the wall surface, press a thin layer of embossing medium through the stencil using gentle pressure. Add more embossing medium to the trowel as needed, until all of the stencil openings are evenly filled.

4 If you want a low-relief design, stop after this layer is applied. If you want a heavy-relief design, add another layer of embossing medium, covering the entire stencil evenly.

5 Remove the stencil slowly, beginning at one corner and pulling it straight away from the wall.

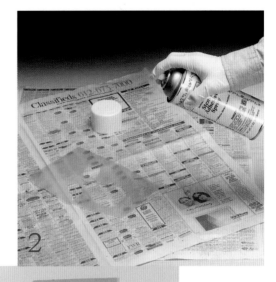

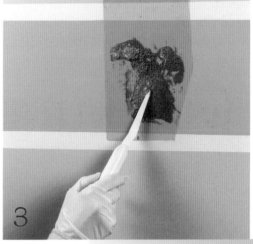

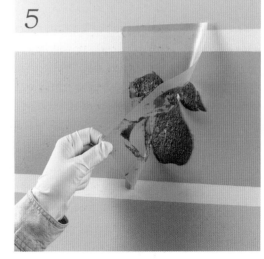

46 Caulking

CAULK DESIGNS ARE limited only by the imagination! Designs consisting of lines and dots are drawn on the wall using tub and tile caulk. When the caulk designs are dry, the wall can be painted in any color desired. The shadows of the raised dots and lines produce subtle patterns.

Caulking can create cheerful flowers, graceful vines, trendy geometric patterns, and other exciting freehand motifs. Dots, swirls, and other simple figures are good for a beginner. This easy technique can add fanciful style to a child's bedroom or bathroom, a laundry room, game room, mudroom, or craft room.

The caulk adheres to the wall better if it is slightly cool when applied. The size of the dots and lines depends on the size of the opening cut in the tip of the caulk tube. For tiny dots and thin lines, cut the tip close to the end. For more substantial dots and lines, cut the tip off deeper. To remove the designs at a later date, scrape them off with a paint scraper, and patch and prime the walls again.

* Painter's masking tape
* Drop cloths
* Paint roller and tray
* Latex primer
* Pencil
* Tub and tile caulk
* Scissors
* Satin latex paint for top coat
* Paintbrush

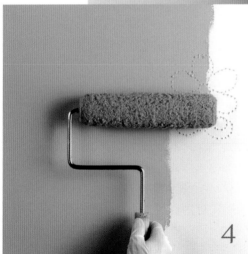

1 Prepare the walls for painting (page 123). Protect the area around the walls with painter's masking tape and drop cloths (page 126). Apply primer to the walls and let it dry completely.

2 Lightly pencil in the design of your choice onto the wall surface. Cut the tip off the caulk tube.

3 Apply dots and lines of caulk over the marked lines, squeezing the tube with even pressure. Stop squeezing and lift the tip from the surface at the end of each line. Using a wet fingertip, smooth down any bumps and tails after 30 minutes. Allow 24 hours for the caulk to dry completely.

4 Apply the top coat to the entire wall.

47 Decoupage

A CENTURIES-OLD art, decoupage is cutting papers and sealing them to a surface. When applied over a beautifully painted base coat, decoupage can transform a wall.

Extremely effective when used in a compact area, decoupage can create a highpoint without overwhelming a space. In a large room, decoupage is a focal point. Black and white prints are traditional favorites for this technique and can be striking when placed over bold back-ground colors. For the background, consider decorative paint finishes such as color washing (page 14), overlaying color (page 16), or double rolling (page 22).

Decoupage must be applied to a smooth wall, as any texture or imperfections will show. Decoupage designs must be printed on lightweight paper so they lie as flat as possible on the wall. It is important that the images be cut out carefully and that all edges are sealed to the wall.

MATERIALS AND TOOLS

- ❖ Painter's masking tape
- ❖ Drop cloths
- ❖ Paint roller and tray
- ❖ Satin latex paint for base coat
- ❖ Desired designs to decoupage
- ❖ Photocopy machine
- ❖ Small, sharp scissors or mat knife
- ❖ Rubber gloves
- ❖ Wallpaper adhesive
- ❖ Foam applicator
- ❖ Stiff paintbrush and natural-bristle paintbrush
- ❖ Flat latex paint for color wash glaze

1 Prepare the walls for painting (page 123). Protect the area around the walls with painter's masking tape and drop cloths (page 126). Apply the base coat and let it dry completely.

2 Make photocopies of designs, enlarging them to the desired size. Cut out the designs using the scissors or the mat knife.

3 Put on rubber gloves. Dilute wallpaper adhesive with an equal amount of water. Apply an even coat of diluted adhesive to the back of a cutout, using the foam applicator.

4 Affix the cutout to the wall, smoothing it from the center outward, using a dry, stiff paintbrush. Allow to dry.

5 Repeat steps 3 and 4 with all the cutouts. If desired, mix the color-washing glaze and color wash the wall, as on page 15.

48 Collage

COLLAGE TRANSFORMS a painted wall with thin, flat materials and sheer, light-colored paper. Water-based sealer coats the application and makes the paper more sheer, revealing the items layered underneath the paper. The result is a translucent, overlapping form and texture.

A great technique for hiding imperfections in walls, the collage process is usually limited to one focal area. The technique can change a bland wall into a personalized work of art!

The base-coat color should be carefully chosen. A muted version will show through after the layers of materials and water-based sealer have been applied. This application is permanent and cannot be successfully removed without damaging the wall. To repaint at a later date, you will need to replace the plasterboard.

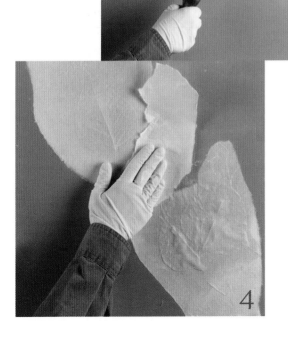

1 Prepare the walls for painting (page 123). Protect the area around the walls with painter's masking tape and drop cloths (page 126). Apply the base coat and allow it to dry completely.

2 Put on rubber gloves. Apply sealer to the wall in a 2-ft. (0.6 m) area using the foam roller. Smooth leaves or other flat materials into place over the wet sealer.

3 Smooth a piece of sheer paper over each collage item. Immediately apply more sealer over the paper, using the foam roller.

4 Apply more pieces of paper in areas not already covered, overlapping the pieces and placing them at various angles, until the entire wall is covered. Allow to dry completely. The papers will nearly disappear, allowing the collage materials to show through.

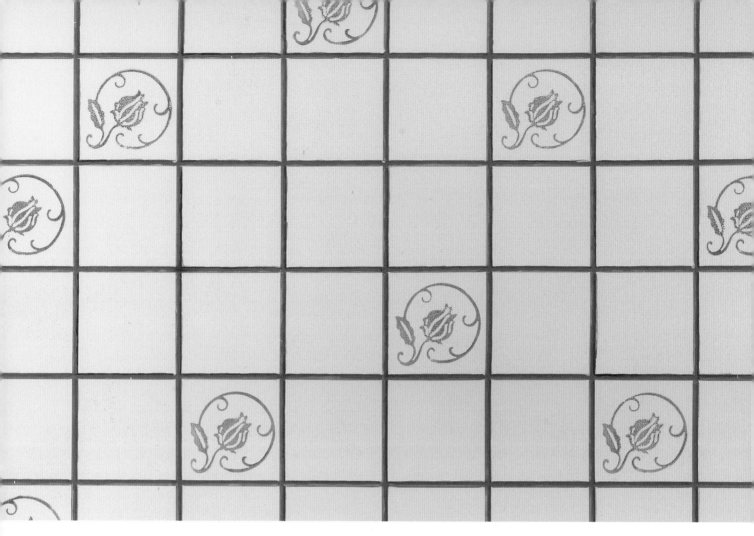

49 Painted Tiles

FOR THE LOOK OF TILE without a large investment of time or money, this hand-painted tiles project is great for the absolute beginner. A square grid of narrow masking tape is secured over the base coat before painting the wall the color of the tiles. The grid becomes the grout between tiles when the tape is removed.

Painted tiles enhance the interior of a kitchen prep space or bathroom and can look festive in a laundry area. Design motifs can be hand painted or stamped onto the tiles to customize them.

Color selection is critical to creating a realistic appearance. Select a base-coat shade in the gray family, as it will become the grout lines between tiles. Various shades of white work well for the top-coat color, providing necessary contrast to the gray grout lines. White shades also help to provide the design contrast needed for the painted tiles to stand out on the wall surface. Bright hues, deep colors, and jewel tones are effective choices for the hand-painted, stamped, or stenciled designs in the centers of individual painted tiles.

MATERIALS AND TOOLS

- ❖ Painter's masking tape
- ❖ Drop cloths
- ❖ Paint roller and tray
- ❖ Gray latex paint for base coat
- ❖ Carpenter's or laser level
- ❖ Pencil
- ❖ Masking tape, 1/4" (6 mm) wide
- ❖ White latex paint for top coat

- ❖ Acrylic paints in black, white, and desired colors for designs
- ❖ Artist's flat paintbrush, 1/4" (6 mm) wide
- ❖ Floating medium
- ❖ Artist's paintbrushes as needed for freehand designs, optional
- ❖ Stencils or stamps for designs, optional
- ❖ Clear sealer

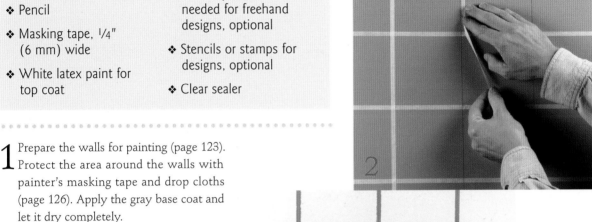

1 Prepare the walls for painting (page 123). Protect the area around the walls with painter's masking tape and drop cloths (page 126). Apply the gray base coat and let it dry completely.

2 Mark a pattern of 4" (10 cm) blocks using the carpenter's level or laser level, and pencil. Apply narrow masking tape over the pencil lines. Make sure the tape seals to the wall well.

3 Apply the white latex paint to the wall. Allow it to dry slightly. Carefully pull the tape off the wall, revealing the "grout lines." Let the paint dry completely.

4 Dip the tip of an artist's flat paintbrush into the floating medium, then into the black paint, and again into the floating medium. Delicately underline the bottom and left side of each square.

5 Hand-paint, stamp (page 102), or stencil (page 106) a design of choice inside each square with the acrylic paints.

6 Apply four coats of clear sealer over the entire painted tile wall surface, allowing the wall to dry completely between coats.

Life is a journey. Travel it well. ~Charishma

50 Words

LETTERS AND WORDS painted on a wall are the most personalized paint technique of all.

Thoughts, quotes, or words that have special meaning can be chosen. A baby's first words can be applied to the walls of a nursery. Quotes from a favorite children's book can be painted over a child's bed. Lettering styles are available in a wide range of options, from contemporary to old world.

The room's existing color scheme should be carefully considered when selecting the colors for the lettering. Monochromatic colors produce a more sophisticated look and can be a stylish accent in rooms with a formal ambience. High contrast between the base-coat color and the colors in the letters produces a bold look that works well for a child's play space or laundry room.

MATERIALS AND TOOLS

- Painter's masking tape
- Drop cloths
- Paint roller and tray
- Latex paint for base coat
- Computer printout of available letter fonts
- Carpenter's or laser level
- Pencil
- Graphite transfer paper
- Acrylic paints in desired colors
- Artist's paintbrushes
- Aerosol flat clear acrylic sealer

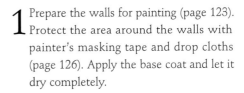

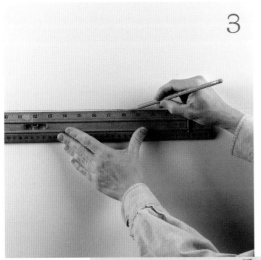

3

4

5

1 Prepare the walls for painting (page 123). Protect the area around the walls with painter's masking tape and drop cloths (page 126). Apply the base coat and let it dry completely.

2 Using the words and font you have selected, print the words from your computer. Determine how large you would like the words to appear on the wall and select the appropriate size for the letters. (If you are unable to print the words large enough on your computer, take the printed words to a copy store and have them enlarged to fit the space of the wall where you want it to go.)

3 Using the pencil and the carpenter's level or laser level, draw a guide line where the words will appear on the wall.

4 Tape a piece of graphite transfer paper to the wall. Place the photocopied words over the transfer paper, aligning them to the marked pencil line. Using the pencil, trace the letters and words.

5 Outline the letters with acrylic paint in the desired color, using a narrow, flat artist's paintbrush. Then fill in the letters, using a slightly wider flat brush. Complete one letter at a time.

6 If the words are in an area that may be touched frequently, spray on several coats of flat clear acrylic sealer, allowing the area to dry between coats.

Painting Basics

The success of your painting project depends greatly on the care that goes into selecting the paints and tools and preparing the walls. They are a crucial part of the process that will reward you with professional results.

All About PAINT

Paint is available in a wide variety of types and finishes, with color choices limited only by your imagination. Whether you want a tough, childproof finish or a soft, sophisticated wash of color, you'll find just the right paint on the shelf of your paint store.

These simple guidelines for choosing paint will help steer you toward the paint products necessary for the look you want.

Types of Paint

Paint falls into two basic categories: water-based or oil-based paint. Both water-based and oil-based paints are available in various sheens, each recommended for different areas of your house.

Virtually all interior painting jobs today—including walls, ceilings, and woodwork—are done using water-based paint, which is commonly called latex paint. Water-based paint is safer for the environment and easier to use than oil-based paint. You can clean up brushes and rollers quickly with soap and water, and just as easily remove spatters from your skin. Latex paint dries quickly on the surface, so you can apply second coats in a few hours. Most latex paints have comparatively mild odors, so room ventilation is less of a concern.

Oil-based paints, also called alkyd paints, give a durable, smooth finish. They do, however, require longer drying times, and, because you must use harsh solvents like mineral spirits or turpentine, cleanup is more complicated.

GLAZES

A glaze is a translucent film applied over a painted surface to create depth and visual texture. By manipulating a glaze with various tools or materials, you can create interesting effects. Glazes are usually a mixture of glazing liquid (which is basically paint binder without the pigment), water, and pigmented paint in proportions suggested by the manufacturer. The resulting glaze has a prolonged drying time, beneficial for creating decorative and faux finishes.

PRIMERS AND SEALERS

Unseen beneath the top paint coat, primers and sealers are nonetheless key ingredients in a quality paint job. Although they usually have very little pigment, these products help cover flaws and ensure that the paint adheres well to the surface. It is usually not necessary to prime a nonporous surface in good condition, like painted wood, painted plaster, or painted drywall.

Primers are available in both water-based and oil-based varieties. Different types are recommended for different jobs.

PAINT	CHARACTERISTICS AND APPLICATIONS
Flat latex	No sheen; for walls and ceilings
Satin latex	Low sheen; for walls, ceilings, trim
Semigloss latex	Slightly glossy sheen; for walls and trim; durable
High-gloss latex	Reflective sheen; for doors, cabinets, trim; washable, durable
Satin-enamel latex	Low sheen; smooth, hard finish; for trim and furniture
Gloss-enamel latex	Very glossy; smooth, hard finish; for trim and furniture
Oil-based enamels	Very glossy sheen; smooth, hard finish; for trim and furniture

FLAT LATEX PRIMER

Used for sealing unfinished drywall or previously painted surfaces, this primer dries quickly so your top coat can be applied on the same day.

DEEP COLOR PRIMER

When you plan to apply a very deep, dark color to your walls, prime first with this type of latex primer. It is designed to be tinted with a color similar to your top coat and will provide better top-coat coverage and appearance.

LATEX ENAMEL PRIMER

Used primarily for sealing raw wood, enamel undercoat closes the pores of the wood and provides for a smooth top finish. Do not use the primer on cedar, redwood, or plywood that contains water-soluble dyes, because the dyes will bleed through the primer.

STAIN-KILLING PRIMER

Available in both alkyd and latex forms, these primers are designed to seal stains like crayon, ink, and grease so they will not bleed through your top coat of paint. Use them to seal knotholes in wood and for cedar, redwood, and plywood that contain water-soluble dyes.

METAL AND MASONRY PRIMER

Designed specifically for use with metal, brick, or cement block surfaces, these latex primers can be used on the interior or exterior of your home.

You may find metal primers for both clean, rust-free metal surfaces and for surfaces where rusting has already occurred. Both types inhibit rusting and allow the top coat to adhere evenly to the metal.

How Much to Buy?

To calculate how much paint you will need to finish your project, use this standard formula. Work in square feet (or square meters).

1. Measure each wall to figure the area:
- height × width = area
- Add the wall totals together for the sum total of wall area.

2. Measure each window and door to figure the area:
- height × width = area
- Add the window and door areas together for the sum total of window and door area.

3. Now subtract the total window and door area from the total wall area:
- wall area − window/door area = total area of the wall space you will need to paint

4. Measure ceilings and floors to figure total area you need to paint:
- length × width = area

Most interior paint products are designed to cover approximately 400 square feet per gallon (36 square meters per 3.56 liters). To figure how many gallons of wall paint you will need, simply divide your total wall area by 400. (Check the paint can label for the manufacturer's coverage recommendation.) Don't forget to double your final amount if you plan to apply two coats.

Drying Times

It is a good idea to estimate how long your painting project will take to complete. While every painter works at a different pace, remember that most projects take more time than originally planned and that preparation and drying times will affect your schedule. As a rule, preparation time takes longer than most people anticipate. If you are planning to work on weekends, for instance, complete your wall preparation on one weekend; the next weekend, you will be ready to move furniture, drape and mask surfaces, and apply paint.

TYPICAL DRYING TIMES		
	WATER-BASED	OIL-BASED
PRIMERS	1–4 hours	4–10 hours; do not recoat for 24 hours
PAINTS	1–4 hours	6–10 hours; do not recoat for 24 hours
STAINS	1–4 hours	6–10 hours; do not recoat for 24 hours

The Right TOOLS

For most home improvement projects, choosing the right tools for the job is half the battle. Painting is no different. So before you grab the first brush or roller cover you spot on the store shelf, bone up on some basics. Because of the abundance of quality, specialized painting products on the market today, you'll have no trouble finding the right tools for your job. With this information, you'll know how to make the best choices.

Rollers

A good roller can be invaluable to your painting project. Inexpensive and efficient, this simple tool can save you time and energy. Rollers are commonly used for painting large wall areas, ceilings, and floors. Two simple components make up the roller: the frame and the cover. Covers are easily changeable, according to the job at hand.

SELECTING A ROLLER FRAME

Choose a standard 9" (23 cm) roller with wire frame and nylon bearings. Check the handle to make sure the molded grip is comfortable in your hand. The handle should also have a threaded end so you can attach an extension handle for painting ceilings and high walls.

SELECTING A ROLLER COVER

Roller covers, or pads, come in either synthetic or natural lamb's wool and are available in a variety of nap thicknesses. In general, synthetic covers are used for water-based paint; lamb's-wool covers are used for oil-based paint. Select roller covers with longer-lasting plastic, rather than cardboard, cores.

- Short-nap roller covers have 1/4" to 3/8" (6 mm to 1 cm) nap. Choose short-nap covers for applying glossy paints to smooth surfaces like wallboard, wood, and smooth plaster.

- Medium-nap roller covers have 1/2" to 3/4" (1.3 to 2 cm) nap. These are commonly called all-purpose covers. They give flat surfaces a slight texture and are a good choice for walls and ceilings with small imperfections.

- Long-nap roller covers have a 1" to 1 1/4" (2.5 to 3.2 cm) nap. Choose long-nap covers for painting textured surfaces, including stucco and concrete block.

Brushes

Paintbrushes fall into two basic categories: natural bristle and synthetic bristle. Do not assume that natural is better, which was once the common wisdom about paintbrushes. In fact, natural-bristle brushes should only be used with alkyd, or oil-based, paint. If natural-bristle brushes are used with water-based paints, the bristles will bunch together. Choose synthetic-bristle brushes for water-based latex paints.

Look for quality. A bargain brush will save you a few dollars up front but may well cost you more in the long run. Invest in a few quality brushes; with proper care, they should last through many paint projects. As a starting point, choose a straight-edged 3" (7.5 cm) wall brush, a 2" (5 cm) straight-edged trim brush, and a tapered sash brush.

A good brush has a strong, hardwood handle. Dense bristles should be flagged, or split, at the ends. Always check to make sure the bristles are attached securely to the handle. If some pull out when you tug, you can expect the bristles to fall out into your paint job. The metal band, or ferrule, should be firmly attached. Inside the bristles, check that the spacer plugs are made of wood, not cardboard, which may soften when wet.

- A 1 1/2" (3.8 cm) trim brush works well for painting narrow woodwork.

- A 2" (5 cm) trim brush works well for painting woodwork and windows.

- Choose a 2" (5 cm) tapered sash brush for painting windows.

- Choose a 4" (10 cm) brush for painting walls and ceilings.

Paint Pads

Paint pads come in a wide variety of shapes and sizes to accommodate many different tasks. Use these foam pads with water-based paints. Small pads with tapered edges are helpful for painting narrow areas like window trim or louvers, while the larger sizes can be used on wall surfaces. Specialty pads are available for painting corners and hard-to-reach areas. Paint pads generally apply paint in a thinner coat than a brush or roller, so additional coats may be necessary.

Preparing the SURFACE

Preparation is the key to a good paint job. Taking the time to repair, clean, and prime your walls will guarantee a longer-lasting paint finish. Because dirt and grease will interfere with a good, smooth paint finish, every surface should be thoroughly cleaned before painting.

Don't rush the preparation process and you'll be rewarded with a beautiful, durable finish once the project is completed.

SURFACE PREPARATION AT A GLANCE		
SURFACE TO BE PAINTED	PREPARATION	PRIMER
Unfinished wood	1. Sand surface smooth. 2. Wipe with tack cloth to remove grit. 3. Apply primer.	Latex enamel undercoat
Painted wood	1. Clean surface to remove grease and dirt. 2. Rinse with clear water; let dry. 3. Sand surface lightly to degloss, smooth, and remove loose paint. 4. Wipe with tack cloth to remove grit. 5. Apply primer to bare wood spots.	Latex enamel undercoat only on areas of bare wood
Unfinished wallboard	1. Dust with hand broom, or vacuum with soft brush. 2. Apply primer.	Flat latex primer
Painted wallboard	1. Clean surface to remove dirt and grease. 2. Rinse with clear water; allow to dry. 3. Apply primer only if making a dramatic color change.	Not necessary, except when painting over spot repairs or dark or strong color; then use flat latex primer
Unpainted plaster	1. Sand surfaces as necessary. 2. Dust with hand broom, or vacuum with soft brush.	Polyvinyl acrylic primer
Painted plaster	1. Clean surface to remove dirt and grease. 2. Rinse with clear water; allow to dry. 3. Repair any cracks or holes. 4. Sand surface to smooth and degloss.	Not necessary, except on spot repairs or when painting over strong or dark colors; then use polyvinyl acrylic primer

Clean the Surface First

To avoid messy streaking, begin washing your walls from the bottom up. While you can use common household cleansers for the job, many professional painters use a TSP (trisodium phosphate) solution.

Wearing rubber gloves, wash with a damp, not dripping, sponge. Rinse thoroughly with clean water. After the surface is dry, sand lightly where need; then wipe the surface with a clean cloth.

As you clean, you will discover any small problems, like cracks or stains, on the surface. Make those repairs before beginning to paint.

Fixing Common Problems

WATER STAINS

Problem: Unsightly water or rust stains require immediate attention because they may indicate a leak somewhere.
Solution: Check for leaking pipes or damaged flashing on the roof. Before you paint, repair the leak. If the wall surface is soft or crumbling, repair the area (pages 125 to 126). To seal and cover a water-stained area that is not otherwise damaged, use a stain-sealing primer that contains shellac. If left unsealed, the stain will eventually show through your new paint job.

COLORED STAINS

Problem: Black marks and other wall stains like crayon or marker are not always easily removed.
Solution: Apply a stain remover to a clean, dry cloth and rub lightly on the stain. Cover any stain that is not completely removed with a stain-sealing primer that contains shellac.

MILDEW AND MOLD

Problem: Because mold and mildew grow in damp areas, check kitchen and bathroom surfaces carefully.
Solution: Test the stain by washing it with water and detergent. If it is mildew, it will not wash away. Wash the area with a solution of one part chlorine bleach to four parts water, which will kill the mildew spores. Scrub with a soft-bristle brush. Then wash the mildew away with a TSP solution, rinse with clear water, and allow the area to dry thoroughly before painting.

PEELING PAINT

Problem: Peeling paint occurs for a number of reasons, and it must be removed before you repaint.
Solution: Scrape away the loose paint with a putty knife or paint scraper. Apply a thin coat of spackle to the edges of the chipped paint, using a putty knife. Allow it to dry. Sand the area with 150-grit sandpaper, creating a smooth transition between bare wall and surrounding painted surfaces. Wipe clean with a damp sponge. Spot-prime the area with polyvinyl acrylic (PVA) primer.

FILLING SMALL NAIL HOLES

1. Using a putty knife or your finger, force a small amount of drywall compound or spackle into the hole, filling it completely. Scrape the area smooth with the putty knife and let dry.

2. Sand the area lightly with 150-grit sandpaper. Wipe clean with a damp sponge, let dry, and dab on PVA primer.

Fixing Popped Drywall Nails

Drywall nails can work themselves loose, either popping through the drywall or creating a small bulge on the surface.

1. Drive a new wallboard screw into place 2" (5 cm) below the popped nail, sinking the head slightly below the wall surface. Be sure the screw hits the stud and pulls the drywall tight against the framing, taking care not to damage the wall surface.

2. Scrape away loose paint or drywall material around the popped nail. Drive the popped nail back into the framing, sinking the head slightly below the drywall surface.

3. Using a drywall knife, cover both the nail hole and the new screw hole with spackle. Sand and prime the patched areas.

Filling Dents and Gouges in Drywall

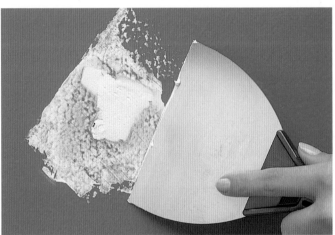

1. Scrape away any drywall paper, using a drywall knife, if necessary. Sand the dented or gouged area lightly. Using a drywall knife, fill the dent or hole with spackle. For deep holes or dents, build up the spackle in layers, allowing each layer to dry before adding another.

2. Sand the patched area with fine-grit sandpaper; seal the area with PVA primer.

Patching Holes in Drywall

1. For a larger problem, cut a neat rectangle around the hole, using a drywall saw. Cut backer strips from drywall or wood; insert them into the opening and hot-glue them to the back of the opening.

2. Cut a rectangular drywall patch slightly smaller than the opening; secure it in place to the backing strips, using hot glue.

3. Apply self-adhesive drywall tape over the cracks; then spackle. After drying, sand the area smooth and apply PVA primer.

4. Self-adhering fiberglass and metal repair patches are available for quick and easy repairs. Simply apply the patch over the hole. Then coat the area with spackle, blending into the surrounding wall. After drying, sand it smooth and apply primer.

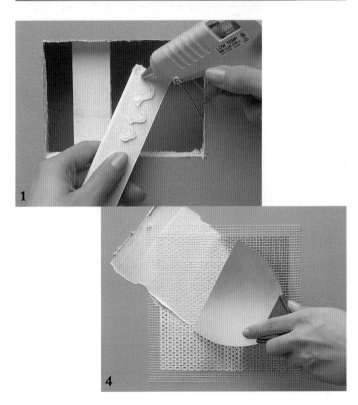

REPAIRING CRACKS IN PLASTER ▶

1. Scrape away any loose plaster or textured surface along the crack. Reinforce the crack with self-adhesive fiberglass drywall tape.

2. Apply a thin layer of joint compound over the taped crack, using a taping knife or trowel. Allow it to dry. Apply a second thin coat, if necessary, to hide the tape edges.

3. Sand the area lightly, using 150-grit sandpaper. Apply PVA primer. Retexture the surface, if necessary, using texturized paint.

REPAIRING HOLES IN PLASTER ▶

1. Gently scrape away any loose material and clean the damaged area. Undercut the edges of the hole where possible.

2. Cut a piece of wire lath to fit the damaged area and staple it to the wood lath. Mix a small amount of patching plaster, following the manufacturer's directions.

3. Using a drywall knife or trowel, apply a thin coat of plaster to the wire lath, working the material under the hole edges.

4. Score a grid pattern into the surface of the patching plaster with the tip of your knife; allow to dry.

5. To apply a second coat, first dampen the area with a sponge; then apply another layer of patching plaster, even with the surrounding wall. Allow it to dry thoroughly.

6. Sand the area lightly, using 150-grit sandpaper. Apply PVA primer. Retexture the surface, if necessary, using texturized paint.

Preparing the Room

Once your repairs have been made, you're almost ready to paint. Take the time now to remove or cover anything in the room that could be spattered by paint as you work. Furniture should be moved into the center of the room and draped with plastic (readily available in large sheets at hardware stores and home improvement centers). Cover floors with canvas drop cloths (paint will not pool up on canvas like it will on plastic), and remove things like switch plates, window and door hardware, duct covers, and wall lights. Use tape to mask off wood moldings.

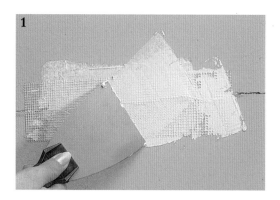

Taking the time to mask and drape thoroughly will save both cleanup time and unnecessary damage to furnishings and fixtures.

TAPING

It is always wise to protect areas like woodwork and window glass that butt up against the surfaces you'll be painting. Taping these areas may save you cleanup time and will ensure a clean, straight finish. To mask woodwork, use painter's tape, which is a wide strip of brown paper with adhesive along one edge (shown at top of page 127). Cut off short lengths of the tape, and, working one section at a time, smooth the adhesive edge onto the woodwork with a putty knife. Keep your edges as straight as possible. The paper edge will stick out past the molding, protecting it from paint spatters.

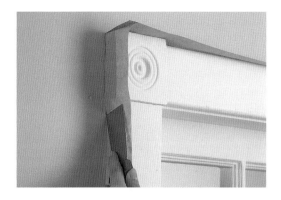

Painter's masking tape (not to be confused with the masking tape used for packages) is specially designed to be applied and removed without damaging painted surfaces. Still, it's best not to leave the tape in place longer than necessary. Carefully removing the tape before the paint dries usually produces a smoother line. Look for these masking tapes in the paint section of your home improvement store. They are available in a wide range of widths and are often colored red or blue.

Cover Light Fixtures

To protect hanging fixtures, unscrew the collar from the ceiling and lower it to expose the rough opening in the ceiling. Then wrap the fixture with a plastic bag.

Draping

When painting the ceiling only, drape your walls with sheet plastic to prevent damage from paint spatters. Use 2" (5 cm) masking tape to hold the plastic sheets to the wall along the ceiling line.

How to PAINT

Using Your Paintbrush

• Transfer some paint from the can into a small paint bucket with a handle. It will be easier to carry with you as you move around the room.

• Double-check your paintbrush. If you are using water-based (latex) paint, you should have a synthetic-bristle brush.

• Don't overload your paintbrush! Dip the bristles only about 2" (5 cm) into the paint. Tap, don't drag, the bristles on the side of the can.

1. Begin painting with horizontal strokes in a back-and-forth manner, using first one side of the brush, then the other. Press the brush against the surface just hard enough to flex the bristles slightly. Always paint from dry areas back into wet areas to avoid lap marks.

2. Smooth the paint evenly across the surface using vertical strokes. Feather, or blend, the edges of your painted area by brushing lightly with just the tip of your brush.

3. Along edges where a wall meets the ceiling or woodwork, use a technique called "cutting in." Hold the brush at a slight angle. Stroking slowly, move the brush slightly away from your edge as you go. This will allow paint to bead up along the straight line of the edge.

Using Your Paint Roller

• Paint surfaces in small sections, working from dry surfaces back into wet paint to avoid roller marks.

• If you do notice roller marks, or lines of beaded paint, beginning to form on your paint job, feather the edges immediately before they dry. Try easing up on the pressure you're applying to the roller to avoid any further roller marks.

• If your paint job will take more than one day, cover the roller tightly with plastic wrap overnight to prevent the paint from drying out. Be sure to run the roller over a piece of scrap material before you begin painting again the next day.

1. Load your roller by dipping it into the paint tray, then rolling it back and forth gently on the textured ramp to distribute the paint evenly. The roller cover should be soaked but not dripping when you start to paint.

2. With the loaded roller settled comfortably in your hand, roll paint onto the surface in smooth, crisscrossing strokes. When working on walls, roll upward on your first stroke to avoid spilling paint.

3. Distribute the paint across the surface using horizontal back-and-forth strokes.

4. Smooth the painted area by lightly drawing the roller down the surface, from top to bottom. Lift the roller at the bottom of each stroke, and then return to the top.

Painting Walls

1. Using a narrow brush, cut in a 2" (5 cm) strip of paint where the walls meet woodwork and ceiling. Begin in the upper right-hand corner if you are right-handed, upper left if you are left-handed. (This helps avoid smearing paint if you accidentally lean into the wall as you work.)

2. Using your roller, paint one small wall section at a time. Work on the wall sections while your edges are still wet. When painting near the cut-in edge, slide the roller cover slightly off the roller. This helps to cover the cut-in edge as much as possible, since brushed paint dries to a different finish than rolled-on paint. Continue painting adjacent wall sections, cutting in with a brush and then rolling wall areas. Work from top to bottom. All finish strokes should be rolled toward the door.

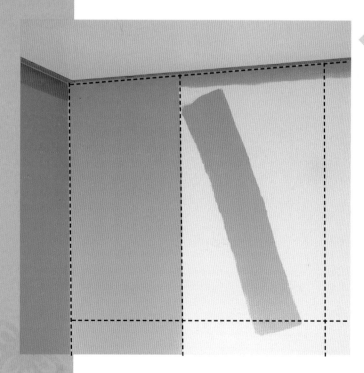